W9-CER-134

STAGE COSTUMES
AND HOW TO MAKE THEM

STAGE COSTUMES

AND HOW TO MAKE THEM

BY

JULIA TOMPKINS

Publishers   PLAYS, INC.   *Boston*

First American edition published by Plays, Inc. 1969
Reprinted 1976

Library of Congress Catalog Card Number: 73–85291
ISBN: 0–8238–0064–4

©
Julia Tompkins
1968

Reproduced and printed by photolithography and bound in
Great Britain at The Pitman Press, Bath

PREFACE

YET another book on Period Costume, in face of an already comprehensive and authoritative bibliography, may appear to be not only superfluous but an impertinence, since I make no pretensions to specialized knowledge. But tagging along behind the architect comes the bricklayer. The artist needs the artisan to translate the idea into the reality; and the designer needs the person who can look at his sometimes nebulous, often downright impossible and unwearable designs, and make them possible and wearable.

Period costume does not need to be accurate down to the last pernickety detail. The costume of the day was often cumbersome and uncomfortable, demanding a degree of management sometimes quite beyond the amateur. It is enough to hint at an epoch, at the same time taking care not to get your dates mixed—you don't wear a hennin with a farthingale. Go to the experts for guidance on *what* and *when*. This book sets out to show *how*.

161977

INTRODUCTION

Now is the winter of our discontent
Made hideous by this bantling's peevish squawk
Of "Mum, I want a costume for the play!"
But how to fashion haught' Plantagenet
From ancient dressing-gown a houppelande
'S beyond me quite, nor can I find receipt
In any pattern book for 'dagged sleeve,'
For 'hennin,' 'liripipe' or 'farthingale,'
Fantastic tirings of these other days—
A plague o' both your houses—and your plays!

THE human frame has not changed through the centuries, and costume is only a variation on a theme.

You won't find a pattern for a houppelande in the pattern-books, but with two basic modern patterns and a good supply of newspapers, you will be able to costume any character from Clytemnestra to Madame Ranevsky.

Once you have acquired the knack of analysing a style and equating it with present-day fashion, the difficulties begin to iron themselves out. For men's costumes, use a pyjama pattern—this is more useful than a shirt pattern, which has the unnecessary complication of a yoke; in addition, the pyjama trousers form the basis of trunk hose and breeches.

For women's costumes, the very simplest dress pattern will suffice. Most of the well-known pattern books feature a "Basic" pattern, consisting of a plain bodice and sleeve, a 4-piece flared skirt, and a straight "shift." The diagrams in this book were adapted from a Men's pyjama (Fig. 1, *A, B, C, D, E, F*) and a Women's Basic (Fig. 2, *A, B, C, D, E, F, and G*) based on size 38 in. chest for the men and 34 in. bust for the women. From practical experience these were found to be the most useful average sizes. It may be thought that a 34 in. bust pattern is on the small side, but it must be remembered that most period costumes depend for their effectiveness on fitting as closely as is consistent with comfort. Also, and of paramount importance, the waist-line must be in the right place. It is easier to allow a little more on the side seam to give a larger bust measurement. Statistics have proved—and I had found out the hard way—that about 75 per cent of Englishwomen are short-waisted. A 34 in. pattern gives a 15–16 in. neck-to-waist measurement and a 4½–5 in. shoulder measurement, both of which are very good averages.

The majority of the sketches in the following chapters have actually been put into practice, and have been worked out to combine effect with economy, at the same time avoiding in the finished costume any suggestion of skimping. The measurements are workable, always allowing for individual variations of height and girth.

When using a pyjama pattern, remember that these jackets are cut on the generous side to allow for freedom of movement. A 38 in. size is excellent for cutting a flowing robe, as, for instance, a full length houppelande of the Plantagenet period, but it is better to use a size smaller when cutting a close-fitting doublet.

The following set of measurements is generally adequate:

Bust (or Chest)

Waist

Hips

Shoulder

Across Back (about half-way between shoulder and armpit)

Neck to Waist (take this measurement at the *back* from spinal knob to natural waist-line)

Waist to ground

Add these two measurements for a full-length robe

Add up to a further 36 in. for a train

Sleeve (outer measurement from point of shoulder to wrist, arm raised and bent)

Shoulder to elbow ⎫
Elbow to wrist   ⎬ Necessary for sleeve as Fig. 35

Measurements must be accurate. Draw the tape fairly tightly, particularly with the men, who are usually swaddled in at least one pullover or woolly waistcoat. Don't be fooled by the belt—that is usually draped round the hips. Just prod firmly about 4 in. higher and say: "Is that where your waist would be if you had one!"

Keep a permanent record of measurements. This saves repeatedly bothering members of the company, and the figures are always on hand to check during actual making. It is also interesting to make a note of each character played by the individual.

In the following chapters, the diagrams will indicate the easiest way of using the basic pattern. My own method was to cut from the original pattern a newspaper replica which could in turn be cut, expanded or modified as necessary. In some cases it is possible to cut from the original pattern just by folding carefully, but any pattern becomes so creased and perforated with constant pinning that the newspaper method is preferable.

Whether you are working from a set of designs worked out by a designer, or simply reproducing from a portrait or a picture in a book, study the costume and break it down into basic sections. Analyse the bodice—is it close-fitting to the true waist-line and tapering to a point in front, as in the Elizabethan era; is it high-waisted, with a diminutive bodice in the Regency style; or, in complete contrast, is the waist-line dropped almost to the hips, as in the early Plantagenet era? However complicated and elaborate a costume may at first seem, this preliminary dissection will give you a rough idea of where to begin to adapt your pattern.

Sleeves, though they may appear excessively intricate, are simple once they have been broken down into individual sections. Experience will show where an overall impression may be given with far less actual cutting and sewing than the picture demands. Slashed sleeves, for instance, are not in reality slashed at all, the illusion being achieved by the application of the contrasting colour. This obviates not only the necessity for a complete under-sleeve to be pulled through the slashings, but also the oversewing and neatening of the actual slashings. The appliqué can later be removed, leaving the original sleeve intact.

The apparently complicated double sleeves often found in early Tudor costume, and the flowing sleeves of the Plantagenet period are also simple to cut.

In the majority of men's costumes, either the tunic or the longer robe cuts out the need for breeches, though these are comparatively workable up to the Victorian era. The slashed and puffed trunk-hose of Shakespeare's day are the easiest of all, being little more than wide, straight pieces of material, with applied contrast, gathered at waist and leg.

While slipshod workmanship is not to be tolerated, too meticulous sewing is unnecessary, and a hindrance to future dismemberment, but the garment must be strong enough to stand up to a certain amount of strain. Any costume sits better for being lined, but it is not necessary to make up the lining separately. A better fit and a firmer garment is achieved if lining and outer fabric are seamed together as though they were a single thickness, particularly where darting is necessary.

Skirts and cloaks hang better, and are more manageable, if weighted. Weighted tape costs about three shillings a yard, but a length of picture chain threaded through the hem is cheaper and achieves the same effect. Small lead weights, like elongated beads, obtainable at any fishing-tackle shop, threaded on string and pinched into place at 6 in. intervals, make efficient ballast for heavier materials.

I make no apology for giving detailed instructions which may sometimes appear to state the obvious; what some people can do with an elementary sewing operation has to be seen to be believed! So the experienced and clever ones can skip the text and get on to the diagrams—though even the expert can sometimes pick up useful tips.

All these operations have been carefully worked out and used with success, always aiming at saving time and unnecessary work. They are offered now to help the harassed and self-confessed "clueless" ones who contrive to get snarled up in this fascinating, frustrating racket. This is a book *for* amateurs *by* an amateur, who had to find out the hard way.

One final injunction—always make certain that a costume is comfortable and secure. Nothing is more distracting than a rasping collar or a slipping hennin.

NOTE ON DIAGRAMS

I have tried to make the diagrams as clear as possible, and have therefore not shown in minute detail the variations between back and front, except where indicated. Most of the diagrams have been worked out with one plan which can be used on either 36 in. or 45 in. fabric, as being the most usual widths. Therefore, a diagram will show either 1¼ yards of 36 in. or 1 yard of 45 in. material. Dotted lines indicate where selvedges join.

The basic pieces of the bought pattern are indicated by shading; the placings have been worked out to use material as economically as possible, but where some waste is unavoidable, the cuttings can be used up for trimming. The quantities quoted are generous averages for adults. For children, the following is a rough guide:

Short Houppelande	Boy's Overcoat +1½ yards 36 in.
Long Houppelande	Boy's Dressing-gown +2–2½ yards 36 in.
Tudor Doublet	Boy's Blazer.
Tudor Hose	Boy's Shorts, doubled.
Saxon, Norman and Plantagenet Gowns	Girl's Nightdress + extra for wide sleeves and train.
Tudor, Stuart, Restoration and Hanoverian gowns	Bridesmaid's dress + 2 yards for sleeves, train, flounce, etc.
Regency etc. and Victorian	Lower Edge measurement (about 3 yards) in 45 in. material (cut bodice along one selvedge). Add up to 1½ yards if using 36 in.

The cutting of velvet requires extra care, and I repeat the warning given elsewhere: *DON'T* cut in a hurry!

Double material is indicated by a small shaded portion at the corner of the diagram.

ACKNOWLEDGMENTS

No book is ever produced single handed, and there are many people without whom this one would never have been completed and published.

Four years with the Croydon Histrionic Society gave me the practical experience which is the foundation of the book, and I must acknowledge the sublime faith of the Committee who lumbered me with the job of Wardrobe Mistress.

I also owe a great deal to the published work of Doreen Yarwood and the late Nevill Truman for guidance on styles and dates of many of the costumes described.

In addition, Miss Joyce Asser's drawings of costumes in wear enhance and bring to life the otherwise dry diagrams.

I offer my most grateful and sincere thanks to all the following: Miss Shirley Munford, who checked the manuscript and diagrams for ambiguities and miscalculations; Mrs. Margaret Cobby, for typing it, and Miss Jean Samson for calling over; Mr. E. A. Edmonds, who made the precision metal templates for the diagrams.

Finally, I owe a very great debt of gratitude to my husband and my mother, who did the chores and the cooking while I banged the typewriter.

Croydon
March 1968

CONTENTS

ILLUSTRATIONS

CHAPTER ONE

SAXON AND NORMAN

SAXON costume is simple, and relies for its effect on the choice of colour and material. The former should be strong, ranging through dark brown, russet, orange and yellow, dark blue, crimson, and green, contrast being provided by banded trimming in a bold, uncomplicated design. The material chosen should give the effect of bulk rather than lightness, with a dull surface. Fur of any kind is a suitable trimming for cloak and sleeve edges, and hems of tunics or gowns.

The predominant feature of men's costumes of this period is the cross-gartered breeches. For these, use the pattern for the pyjama trousers (Fig. 1, piece (*E*)), cross-gartered with coloured webbing about 1½ in. wide. Allow, on average, about 2 yards of webbing for each leg. Mark 3 in. either side of the half-way point, and stitch to trouser seams to form a strap under the instep. Run elastic through the bottom hem for a close fit at the ankle; thread strong elastic at the waist.

Cut the tunic to a length just above the knee, using pieces (*A*) and (*B*) (Fig. 1), as indicated in Fig. 4. Use piece (*D*) (Fig. 1), for the plain inset sleeve (this is more economical than a Magyar sleeve). The average pyjama sleeve will be found to be somewhat wider than is necessary, so a small pleat can be made from shoulder to wrist, and the pattern will then fit on 36 in. material.

Allow an average of 4 yards of 36 in. material for the tunic, and 2½ yards of 36 in. material for the trousers, for which cotton sheeting is suitable. (Make up in accordance with pattern instructions, omitting the fly.) This yardage is based on a 38 in. pyjama pattern; if a smaller costume is required, consult the amounts stated on the pattern envelope, and deduct double the measurement from waist to floor as representing the trousers.

Place centre front of tunic pattern to fold; a centre back seam does not matter.

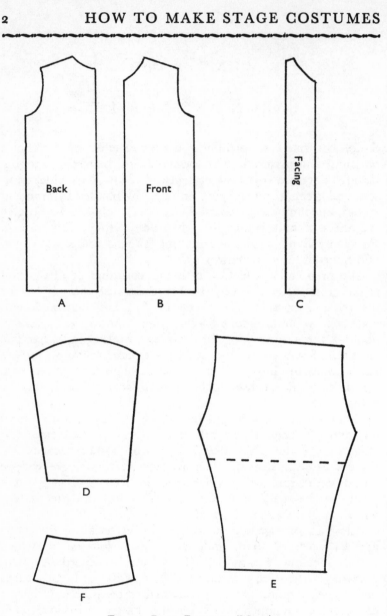

FIG. 1. BASIC PATTERN (MALE)

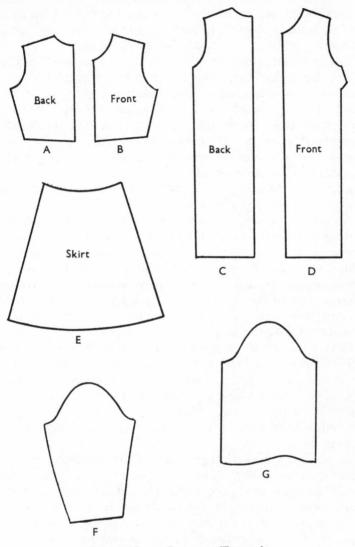

FIG. 2. BASIC PATTERN (FEMALE)

NOTE: The front pattern piece of a pyjama jacket will make allowance for the revers and buttoned overlap. To find true centre front, fold pattern back to line of small perforations indicating position of buttonholes (about 1½ in.).

Leave a 6 in. opening at the back, and finish with hook and eye at the back of the neck. If it is intended to trim the neckline with a contrasting ornamental band, put this on first, before joining shoulder seams. Machine on the outer edge first, and reduce to fit neck by means of tiny pinch pleats every two inches (in the same way as a flared hem is reduced). Use the same trimming for bottom hem-line, and by way of variation, leave open about 12 in. of side seam and continue trimming on each edge, mitring the corners. Draw in at the waist with a plain girdle or belt.

As an alternative, make the tunic with an elbow-length, close-fitting sleeve, trimmed to match hem, and insert a long sleeve in a contrasting colour to simulate the under-tunic which was actually worn. There is no need to make this sleeve separately, since extra bulk is always to be avoided. Merely slash at the "short-sleeve" point which is indicated in most pyjama sleeve patterns, and cut lower piece in contrasting material. Cover the join with the trimming.

Cloaks can be as voluminous as the wardrobe fund allows. Bolton sheeting or hessian are inexpensive and suitable, both being obtainable 72 in. wide. Allow 1¾ yards, and cut as Fig. 5(*A*). Reverse one piece and join centre back seam *on bias*—this hangs better. Make 6 in. darts on shoulder as marked. Trim with contrast banding and fasten with a chunky buckle.

Cloaks are a basic, integral part of the wardrobe, and it is worth spending a little more time and money on them. They should be fully lined, and unbleached linen is most suitable, being neutral in colour and available in several widths— 72 in. is preferable. Cut the lining to the same pattern and make up in the same way. Place the two sections together, right sides together, and machine top and bottom edges. Press all seams open, and turn right side out. Match the two centre back seams, and pin or tack together. Now turn each section back on itself so that the two facing raw seam edges are uppermost; tack these two edges together close to the

FIG. 3. SAXON MAN

original seam—do not pull the thread too tightly otherwise it will snap with the slight drag on the bias. If a swing-needle machine is available, use the maximum swing and stitch size. Repeat the operation on the other edges of the centre back seam. Weight the lower edge, either with picture chain or small fishing weights. The two sets of selvedge edges can now be machined together, all raw edges being neatly concealed. The decorations need only be tacked on, thus allowing for easy removal.

For a more voluminous cloak cut as in Fig. 5(B) and allow 4 yards of 72 in. or 5 yards of 54 in. material. Here again, the essential feature is the bias-cut centre back seam, the sides being on the straight of the grain. It is but too easy to reverse these edges; with the sides on the bias, the hem will droop, the back will hang flat instead of in graceful flutes, and the

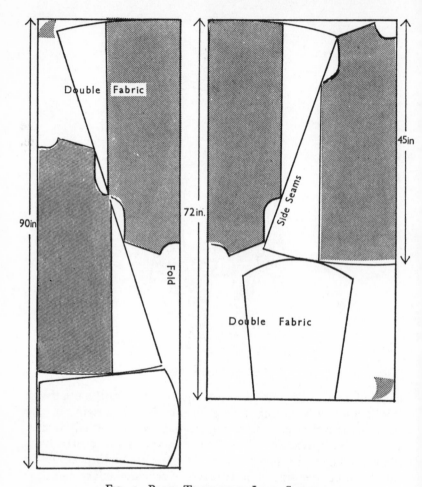

FIG. 4. PLAIN TUNIC WITH LONG SLEEVES

Left: Using 2½ yards of 54 in. material; *Right:* Using 2 yards of 72 in.
material or 4 yards of 36 in. material

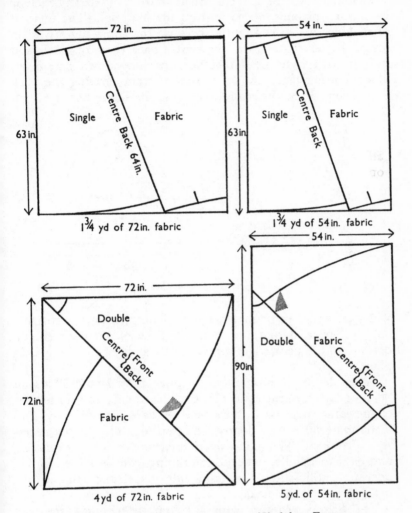

FIG. 5. CLOAKS: (A) *above*, PLAIN: (B) *below*, FLARED

(A) *Top left:* Using 1¾ yards of 72 in. fabric; *Top right:* Using 1¾ yards of 54 in. fabric; (B) *Bottom left:* Using 4 yards of 72 in. fabric; *Bottom right:* Using 5 yards of 54 in. fabric

whole effect will be ruined. So it is worth taking particular care when placing the pattern on the material. The method of making up varies slightly, because the front edges will no longer be selvedges. Join the centre back seam of cloak and lining; with right sides together, machine down one front, along bottom hem and up the other front, leaving the neck edge open. Press the seams open (use the sleeve board, which

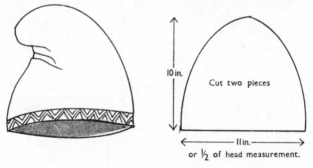

FIG. 6. SAXON CAP

will pass easily through the neck opening). Turn right side out; for extra strength, machine a piece of narrow webbing double, to the neck edge, turn inwards and fell the lining into place.

When the Saxon was not fighting, he wore a kind of Phrygian "cap of liberty," cut as in Fig. 6. This can be of thin felt, or of the same material as the cloak. A lining is necessary, and if the material is very floppy, an interlining gives it the necessary firmness. The non-woven interfacings are inexpensive and easy to handle, and the interlining can be joined in one operation. Slip-stitch the lining into place, and trim with a band to match the cloak.

The Saxon peasant wore a rough, untrimmed tunic of drab, fustian material; ragged edges and an occasional jagged tear underline his poverty and servitude.

Women's costumes are equally simple, being no more than the loose tunic held in place by a girdle. Again, the effect depends on colour and texture, but more contrasts are possible, since the Saxon lady wore two main garments, both of which were in evidence. Her under-gown, or kirtle, was a plain,

FIG. 7. SAXON WOMAN

loose tunic reaching to the floor; it had full-length, close-fitting sleeves long enough to be drawn over the hands in cold weather—otherwise they were pushed up, rather in the same way as we now do with the sleeves of cardigans. Over the kirtle was worn the gunna—the word has become gown over the centuries. This was also a tunic, shorter than the kirtle, about twelve inches from the ground. The sleeves were shorter and wider, forerunners of the wide hanging sleeves of the later Plantagenet period.

To cut down on expense and work, and to reduce bulk, insert the undersleeve at the armhole. The kirtle is made separately as a waist slip, and is thus available as an underskirt in future productions.

Fig. 8 shows the method generally used for cutting a tunic, gown, etc., to utilize the material to the best advantage and to obtain the maximum fullness.

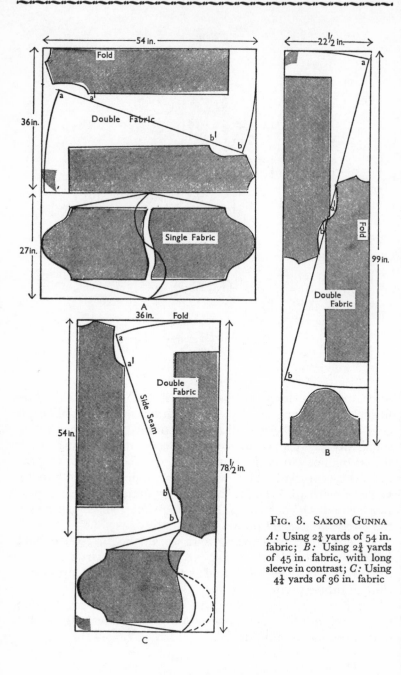

FIG. 8. SAXON GUNNA

A: Using 2¾ yards of 54 in. fabric; *B:* Using 2¼ yards of 45 in. fabric, with long sleeve in contrast; *C:* Using 4¼ yards of 36 in. fabric

First cut right along the diagonal line *a–b*, then from points *a'* and *b'*, hollow out armholes from underarm to shoulder. Thus *a'–b* becomes the side edge of the front, and *b'–a* becomes the side edge of the back. The minor variations at points *a'* and *b'* do not matter.

It will frequently be found impossible to cut back *and* front without a seam, and with some materials a seam will occur back and front—when using 36 in. material, for instance. With some lay-outs, too, a seam will be necessary down the centre of the sleeve (Fig. 16). In actual wear, however, this will not be noticeable from the audience.

For the gunna, use Pieces (*C*), (*D*) and (*G*) of basic pattern (Fig. 2), adapted as in Fig. 8 (*A*), (*B*) and (*C*).

Note on cutting wide sleeves: Fold the remaining rectangle (27 in. × 54 in.) in half; cut along the lines of the underarm seams and tops, then open out flat and mark with chalk the curved dividing line.

The two semi-circles—which may vary in depth from 5–7 in., must be equal. Make a pattern in newspaper, using a 13½ in. diameter.

36 in. material allows for a longer fall, as indicated by broken line as in Fig. 8(*C*).

It is worth while to cut and retain a brown-paper pattern of this hanging sleeve, as it is used, with variations of width and length, right through to the end of the Tudor period.

Follow the instructions given for assembly of these double sleeves in the chapter on Plantagenet costume.

The over-sleeve can also be plain and short, with the lower edge trimmed with a band of embroidery.

Cut the underskirt as in Fig. 9, using either 36 in., 44 in., or 54 in. material. These lay-outs give a fuller hemline and eliminate waist-line bulk. The maximum waist measurement is about 36 in. and this can be reduced by elastic or darts. Leave one selvedge seam open about 7 in. for placket—a zip is not necessary.

Trim the neckline and lower hem with bands of embroidery. Chunky jewellery is appropriate, with cabochon-cut stones rather than diamanté; the same type of "jewels" can be worked into the fillet which was worn to keep the head covering in place, and the "head rail" or veil may be as voluminous and

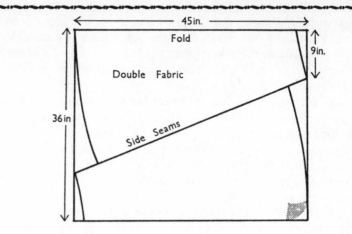

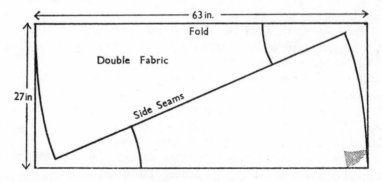

FIG. 9. KIRTLE

Top: Using 2½ yards of 36 in. or 2 yards of 45 in. fabric; *Bottom:* Using
1¾ yards of 54 in. fabric

filmy as you please. The young, unmarried women wore their
hair in two long plaits, twined with bright ribbons; sometimes
the ends were tucked into jewelled tags like aiguillettes, which
can be made from painted buckram. Eight of these "ice-cream
cones" can be cut from one circle of 6 in. radius.

The older women concealed their hair, and the head rail, a
rectangle about 2½ yd. × 27 in., was swathed round the neck,
the loose end falling to the shoulder, kept in place by the fillet.

Footwear for the women is no problem, since soft, heel-less,

FIG. 10. NORMAN MAN

kid or plastic slippers cost so little and are available in a very wide range of colours.

For the men, an unobtrusive slipper in a dark colour or a plain, unlaced shoe with side gussets is probably preferable to a clumsy attempt at authenticity. Peasants can wear crude hessian sandals which are hardly more than circles of material lashed into place with webbing. "Props" can take care of the military in the matter of helmets and breastplates, etc.

There was no dramatic switch of fashion with the Norman Conquest. Saxon and Norman had been shuttling to and fro across the Channel for decades, so the change of government brought only minor variations in its train.

The Saxon peasant exchanged Harold for William, and carried on as before. His Norman counterpart probably differed only in language.

The changes to be noted are mainly the lengthening of the

Fig. 11. Norman Man Wearing Cloak

men's tunics, which now reached to the ankles, with deeper, more ornate banding; cloaks became more voluminous, and were worn with the fastening on the right shoulder. The women played around with sleeves, and called the kirtle a chemise (it was usually of white linen); the gunna became the gown.

For all practical purposes, therefore, the same methods can be applied as have already been described, merely making the garments longer and fuller. The length will probably vary between 54 in. and 60 in., and the heavy trimming will eliminate the need for a deep hem. In some cases 54 in. material can be cut widthways, using the same yardage and layout as in Fig. 8 since the men's sleeves had by now become wider. For a longer tunic, follow the layout in Fig. 13.

The cloak was mostly worn with the straight edges hanging from the right shoulder and the former centre-back draped instead over the left arm (Fig. 11). (This type of cloak can

FIG. 12. NORMAN WOMAN

easily be converted into a skirt for a later production.) Allow
3 yards of 72 in. or 4 yards of 54 in. fabric. When using 72 in.
material cut the cloak in one piece; with 54 in. fabric join the
selvedges on the line (b)–(c). It will be seen from the diagram
that the curve (c)–(d) has been considerably flattened, to
eliminate the tendency of the material to drop on the bias
line (a)–(e) (Fig. 14).

The remaining off-cuts of material are sufficient to make
shoulder-capes and hoods such as would be worn by retainers
or peasants. Cut as indicated on the diagram, and join the
remaining triangles into squares for the hood.

Trim the cloak with bold contrasting embroidery or appliqué—the latter can be cut from felt and stuck on with
Copydex.

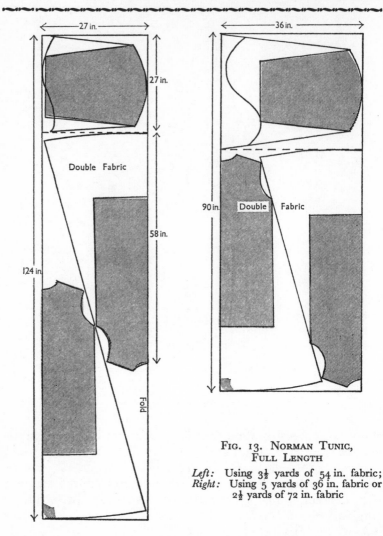

FIG. 13. NORMAN TUNIC,
FULL LENGTH

Left: Using 3½ yards of 54 in. fabric;
Right: Using 5 yards of 36 in. fabric or
2½ yards of 72 in. fabric

Women's gowns were similar in style and cut to those already described earlier in this chapter. The main innovation was the flowing sleeve which became so exaggerated as to require to be knotted to avoid tripping the wearer. This seems a point where strict emulation of the period would cause some embarrassment in actual stage wear, and is better omitted. An attractive sleeve need not be longer than, say 36 in., a good

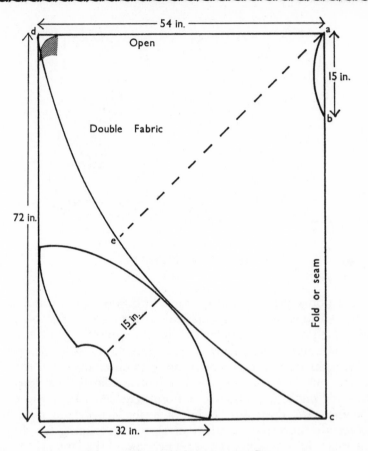

FIG. 14. NORMAN CLOAK WITH CAPE

average being the measurement taken from the wearer's elbow to the ankle.

The close-fitting undersleeve of the chemise is cut and inserted as already described. The outer sleeve is cut in two pieces, the upper section being similar in length and width to that on a short-sleeved blouse, and the lower section, with a contrasting lining, cut as in Fig. 15. Make a pattern from a double page of newspaper folded top to bottom and trimmed to the measurements on diagram.

Assemble gown in the following order: join shoulder seams;

2

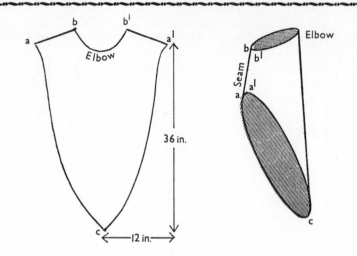

FIG. 15. LOWER SLEEVE, NORMAN

attach upper sleeve; join underarm and side seams (this is not a close-fitting garment, so meticulous fitting is unnecessary—merely check that shoulder seams are correct). Join *a–b* to *a'–b'* on outer (lower) sleeve and on lining. Press seams open. With right sides facing, match lining to outer sleeve all round curved outer edge *a–c–a'*, and stitch with a fairly loose tension (to avoid puckering) about ⅜ in. from edge. Pull lining through opening *b–b'*, press outer edge of lower sleeve, and tack together the curved raw edges of sleeve and lining at elbow opening. Join to upper sleeve. The seam of the lower sleeve is *not* matched to the under-arm seam of the upper sleeve, but to a point about 3 in. towards the front, on a line with the wearer's thumb. Tack and fit before machining, to ensure that sleeve hangs correctly. This is another point where meticulous workmanship is unnecessary; the lining *ought*, of course, to be turned inwards and hand-stitched over the raw edges, but all that takes time and doesn't show, so don't bother. If the material is inclined to fray, overlock, or oversew raw edges by hand.

Finish off with a band of embroidery or braid round the point where upper and lower sleeve join.

Most of the suitable materials for this period are 54 in. or

72 in. wide, and this makes cutting easier and more economical, particularly for the full length gowns and cloaks. Layouts are also given for 36 in. material where feasible, since the extra seams are concealed in the folds.

The gunna is a loose-fitting robe which can be cut from a plain nightdress pattern (without a yoke). Most pattern books have one which includes a long full sleeve gathered into the wrist, and this is the most useful, needing very little modification to adapt to the wide hanging sleeve.

NOTE: All the layouts in this chapter are worked out on the assumption that the fabric used is reversible.

CHAPTER TWO

PLANTAGENET

The Plantagenets ruled England and a large part of France for 300 years, and while it would be an over-simplification to suggest that fashion did not change during the whole period, there is, nevertheless, a basic line which remained fairly constant.

In the earlier reigns the cut and type of garment did not differ very much from the Norman. Men still wore tunics of varying lengths, though these had more fullness than hitherto. This effect is achieved by allowing extra width and gathering into a flat, embroidered band at the neck. The basic pattern is positioned about 6 in. from the centre fold, thus allowing an extra 12 in. back and front (Fig. 16). This tunic may either have a short sleeve over a close-fitting contrast sleeve, or the wider sleeve shown in Fig. 13.

In John's reign the Surcote was introduced. This was a plain, sleeveless over-tunic, with no fullness, slit to the waist for ease of movement, and designed originally to be worn over mail or armour to protect it from rust. Use the basic pattern without any alteration, other than for length.

The most notable differences, however, were in materials. The returning Crusaders brought back rich, shining fabrics such as silk, gauze and damask, with interwoven gold threads.

In the reign of Edward II tights came into the picture. The tunic—now called a Cotehardie—became abbreviated and tight fitting, and the belt, highly ornamental and often with a small square hanging pouch, slipped downwards from the waist to the hips.

There is nothing complicated in the cutting of the cotehardie, which is simply the basic pattern, varying in length from hip-length to just below the knee. However, since this must be a really good fit, and pyjama patterns are always on the loose side, it is better to use a size smaller in order not to waste material in cutting away the surplus. The sleeve also should fit closely, so it is essential to check individual measurements of

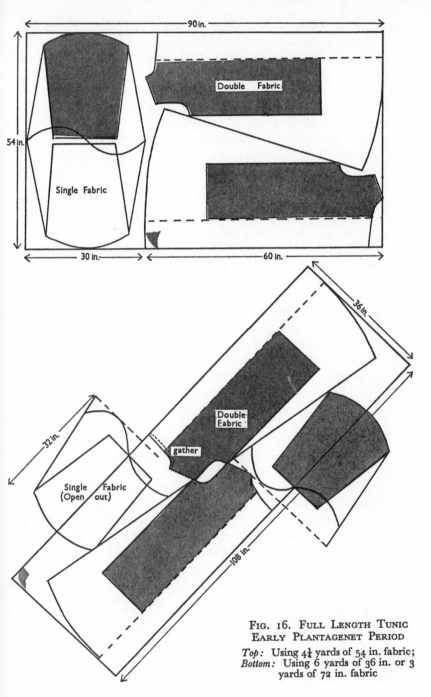

90 in.

54 in.

Double Fabric

Single Fabric

30 in.

60 in.

36 in.

Double-Fabric

gather

32 in.

Single Fabric
(Open out)

108 in.

Fig. 16. Full Length Tunic
Early Plantagenet Period

Top: Using 4¼ yards of 54 in. fabric;
Bottom: Using 6 yards of 36 in. or 3
yards of 72 in. fabric

21

upper- and forearm with the sleeve pattern, and make the necessary adjustment before cutting. Even better, though a little more trouble, is to use the two-piece sleeve from a jacket pattern, tightening on both seams and leaving an opening at the wrist. With this type of sleeve, it is necessary to machine the side seam before inserting sleeve, because the underarm and side seams do not coincide.

As always, cloaks were worn, and being divested of the clutter of the long tunic, can look very effective with a contrasting lining. In shape they can be the same as the Norman cloak, but fastened in front instead of on the shoulder. The short cape and hood were also worn.

It is worth while, when planning a production, to go to the reference books and study the sumptuary laws, which set very definite limits on what might and might not be worn according to status. This affords guidance in deciding what a particular character shall wear, and is a useful indication to an audience of the rank and importance of the part.

Men wore the houppelande; this varied from full length to the most abbreviated, which was hardly more than a bodice with a frill. These are perhaps the easiest costumes to cut. The full length houppelande, appropriate to the more elderly or middle-aged role, is virtually an elaborate dressing-gown, worn open or closed in front, belted or loose.

The effectiveness of the short houppelande depends on accurate fitting at the waist, and although it can be cut all in one piece, it should be mounted on a closely fitted lining, with the fullness pleated into the waist and sewn firmly in position.

Use pieces (*A*) and (*B*) of Fig. 1, adapted as shown in Fig. 19 for the short houppelande. Cut the long robe as in Fig. 13, allowing an extra ½ yard of 54 in. and ¼ yard of 72 in. material to make up the difference in length—this robe may be ground length or even have a small train at the back, but keep the front to instep length, to avoid the possibility of tripping the wearer.

Depending upon the thickness of the material, the garment may be interlined, but it is not necessary to make the lining up separately; tack the lining for each piece to the material round all its edges and make up as one piece. (This instruction

FIG. 17. SHORT HOUPPELANDE

applies to any lining, unless specifically mentioned to the contrary.)

The short houppelande is effective when made without a seam in the centre front, with the front of the garment inter-lined with wadding and quilted from shoulder to waist. Cut and fit the inner lining first; then, before joining the side seams, lay the garment flat and tack pleats from shoulder to waist firmly on to the lining.

NOTE: Join seams in the following order: Shoulder seam—press open. Insert sleeves, and always machine together *with the main garment uppermost.* The machine foot will then ride more easily over smooth fabric, and will not become fouled

FIG. 18. LONG HOUPPELANDE WITH DAGGED SLEEVE

with pleats, gathers, etc. Lastly, tack side and underarm seams, and fit costume before finally machining.

If the full length houppelande, appropriate to the older characters, is to be worn open down the front, cut a matching facing from piece (C) of Fig. 1. If a closed front is preferable, so saving the need for tights, the opening, which should still be faced, need not be cut lower than the waist. Either costume can be worn with or without a belt or ornamented girdle, and fur edgings to fronts and sleeves add greatly to the richness of the appearance.

Sleeves were perhaps the most striking feature of this era. When houppelandes were at their shortest, the wide over-sleeves were sometimes so long that they were tied in a loop

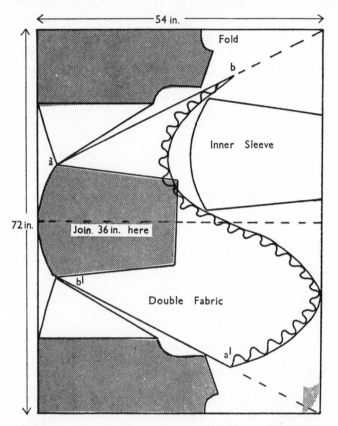

FIG. 19. SHORT HOUPPELANDE WITH DAGGED SLEEVE

6 yards of 36 in. fabric + 3 yards contrast for lining; or 4 yards of 54 in.
fabric + 1½ yards contrast; or 3 yards of 72 in. fabric + 1 yard contrast.

at the back. They were capable of infinite variation, and
Figs. 19 to 22 show three examples. With Figs. 19 and 22, *top
right*, wear a tight fitting undersleeve. Figure 22, *bottom*, is a bag-
sleeve, the fullness gathered into a plain cuff.

For the undersleeve, use piece (*D*) of Fig. 1 (or a two-piece
jacket sleeve, as previously suggested). Tighten on under-arm
seam to fit the individual, leaving open the last 4 inches and
fasten at wrist with hooks and eyes. Trim opening with
buttons if desired.

Fig. 19 shows how to use the plain sleeve pattern as a guide to cutting the wide over-sleeve, which should be lined with a contrast. Fig. 22, *top left*, shows how *not* to cut this sleeve, even though by doing so you economize slightly on material. But unless you are prepared to modify the sleeve

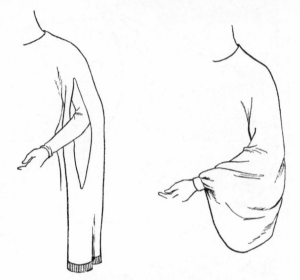

FIG. 20. STRAIGHT HANGING SLEEVE   FIG. 21. BAG SLEEVE

head and also forgo the convenience of having underarm and side seams continuous, you will find that the sleeve will not hang properly and will cause unnecessary irritation to the wearer.

If you decide to have dagged edges, use a U-curve rather than a sharp vandyke, which is always difficult, particularly with a loosely-woven material. To assemble, first join bottom edge of sleeve to bottom edge of lining, right sides together. Trim turnings carefully to about $\frac{1}{4}$ in. and snip on inward curves. Press seam open, turn right side out and press again.

NOTE: This is one of the instances in which the lining should *not* be joined in one operation with the main garment, as the raw edges will show in wear.

Having joined shoulder seams, insert outer sleeve. Tack from hem to underarm, continue down underarm sleeve seam,

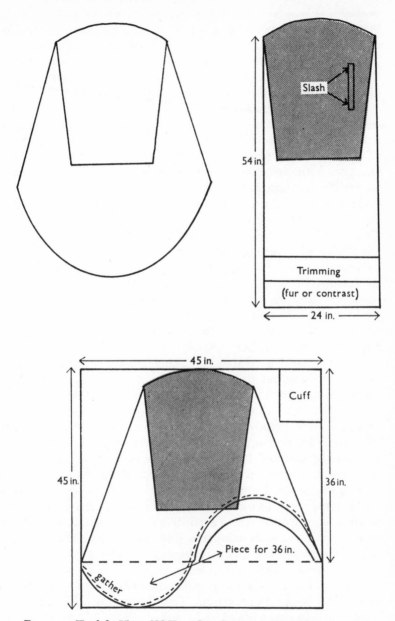

FIG. 22. *Top left:* How *NOT* to Cut Sleeve; *Top right:* Hanging
Sleeve; *Bottom:* Bag Sleeve. This can be used instead of the
Dagged Sleeve in Fig. 19.

and along the underarm seam of lining. Fit costume at this stage. (*In practice, it is only the short houppelande which needs this final fitting*, since the full length robe either hangs loosely or is drawn in with the belt, and the only point which needs to be checked is the width of the shoulder seam.)

Now machine the seam in one continuous operation—*before* inserting the undersleeve. Draw the lining inwards and sew into place round armhole. Finally, join the underarm seam of the under-sleeve, and tack it in firmly by hand, rather than struggle with an almost unmanageable amount of material under the machine foot.

The same basic method can be used to assemble the straight hanging sleeve in Fig. 22. This is a useful and economical design, suitable for older characters. For royalty and nobility, the slash and lower edge of the sleeve can be trimmed with fur, velvet or other rich looking fabric; less exalted characters such as major-domos, clerks, citizens and the like, would wear sober colours, relieved only by a lighter shade of the same basic colour. If a fairly substantial material is used, lining is unnecessary, and the lower edge can be finished with a contrasting trim about 6 inches wide.

Make the slit before attaching the sleeve to the garment. The slit should be about 10 in. deep, positioned to fit the individual —from 5 in. above to 5 in. below the elbow. Mark it carefully before slashing. Cut a rectangle of contrasting fabric about 16 in. × 10 in., draw a chalk line down the centre and mark off 4 in. from the top and bottom. With the *right* side of the contrasting material to the *inside* of the sleeve, pin the contrast in position as marked, and machine-stitch it ⅜ in. on either side of the centre line, rounding off the top and bottom ends or squaring them as indicated in the diagram. Slash down the chalk line, clip the ends carefully (if the material is inclined to fray, paint it with colourless nail varnish and allow to dry before clipping), and draw it through to the right side. Turn under and top stitch to the sleeve.

Cut another strip of contrast the same width as the end of the sleeve and about 13 in. deep. Turn in ½ in. on the top edge, place the hemmed edge on right side of the sleeve 6 in. from the bottom edge, and top stitch. Proceed as before, finally stitching the under-arm seam and continuing the stitching beyond the

main sleeve to the end of the contrast, then fold the surplus
back inside the main sleeve and slip-stitch or Copydex it in
place.

The bag sleeve in Fig. 22 is cut in the same way as the outer
sleeve in Fig. 19 (without the dagged lower edge and lining)
and the fullness is gathered into a plain narrow cuff. Make a
narrow ($\frac{1}{4}$ in.) hem on the last 3 in. of the under-arm edges, and
attach the cuff, which is a straight piece of material 7 in. ×
10 in. (The cuff pattern of a man's shirt will serve.) Pleat or
gather in the fullness, which should not be excessive, *befoer*
doubling and sewing the ends of the cuff, being careful to leave
$\frac{5}{8}$ in. free at either end of cuff for turnings. Machine the right
sides together with the plain piece uppermost. Then fold the
cuff in half, machine the ends, turn right side out and hem free
edge over gathers. Insert sleeve as before, running seam off
the turning about $\frac{1}{2}$ in. beyond end of narrow hem. Close the
cuff with hooks and eyes or strong press studs—*two* on each
cuff are essential.

Necklines may be finished in various ways. On a short
houppelande, no more than a plain, "mandarin" type collar
about 2 inches wide, of the same colour as the undersleeves, is
necessary. Cut a straight strip of material 5 in. wide and as
long as the individual player's normal collar size, plus 1 in. for
turnings. Fold in half, machine the short edges, turn to the
right side and press. Attach to the round neck of the garment
on the right side, taking in both raw edges of the neckband,
turn all raw edges downwards and press. Run a further row
of machine stitching along the edge of the main garment—this
will prevent the neckband, which may be stiffened if necessary,
from flopping outwards. Trim down the raw edges and if the
material frays, finish with cotton bias binding or with over-
locking if a swing-needle machine is available. (This again
is not the *proper* way to do the job—the raw edges *ought* to be
pressed upwards and the inner edge of the neckband felled over
them. But that can lead to a clumsy, bulky neckline when
using thick material, and in any case when you're working
against time, you have no time for absolute perfection.) The
same collar, cut about double the width and edged with a
narrow strip of fur, makes an elegant and becoming finish to
either a long or short houppelande; similarly, the graceful

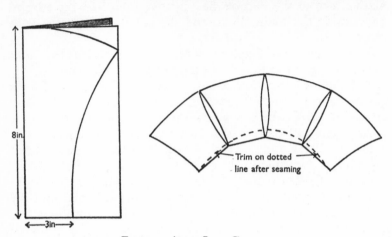

FIG. 23. ARUM LILY COLLAR

"arum-lily" style collar. To make a pattern for this collar, take a sheet of paper 8 in. square, and fold in half. Mark curves as indicated in Fig. 23 and trim to shape. Open out, and cut four pieces for the under-collar of the same material as the main garment; the upper collar may be of contrast to match either the sleeve linings or the under-sleeve. Cut four pieces of whichever colour is selected.

The collar must be interlined; any of the non-woven interlinings such as Vilene are suitable, but if cost is a vital factor and the costume is only to be used for four or five performances, newspaper (about four thicknesses) or thick brown paper will serve. Cut four interlining pieces and tack to the under-collar. Join the centre back and two side seams. Make upper collar in the same way. Place the two sections together, right sides facing, and machine round outer edge on three sides. Trim neck edges as indicated in diagram taking $\frac{3}{4}$ in. from centre back, tapering to nothing at front edge. (This gives a curve which will marry easily with neck of garment, and eliminates the necessity for making two slightly different pattern pieces which can very easily get joined up in the wrong order.) Now trim the points and turnings, and tack fine ribbon wire or soft galvanized wire round outer edge. Bend back last $\frac{1}{2}$ in. of wire and cover with sticking plaster. (*Don't*

FIG. 24. FITTED PLANTAGENET GOWN

use millinery wire; it is too stiff and unmanageable, and the
points always manage to work through the material.) Turn
right side out, and attach to garment in the same way as
straight collar. This collar must fit snugly to the neck and must
have a fastening, otherwise it will flop backwards. The
wired edges can then be bent into a gentle outward curve.

Women began to be aware that their hitherto rather sloppy
garments could become much more exciting if they were
laced tightly to emphasize the figure, and denunciations from
pulpits fell on deaf ears. The Plantagenet era accordingly
offers a fascinating variety of some of the most becoming styles
in history. There is a fairy-tale quality and a gracefulness of
line, without the stiffness and clutter which developed in the
Tudor and Stuart costume. Skirts were voluminous and
flowing, hennins soared, gossamer veils floated, and even the
most homely features were enhanced by the wimple, with its

FIG. 25. PLANTAGENET GOWN WORN WITH SURCOTE

kindly concealment of the double chin and subtle disguise of the too plump jowl.

This is one of the easiest periods to copy, and the current sheath line serves with very little modification. Using pieces (C), (D) and (F) of the basic pattern, cut as indicated in Fig. 26. For the sake of economy of material the sweep of the small train can be obtained by inserting in the centre back seam a triangular "fish tail" about 32 in. long and 16 in. wide, the

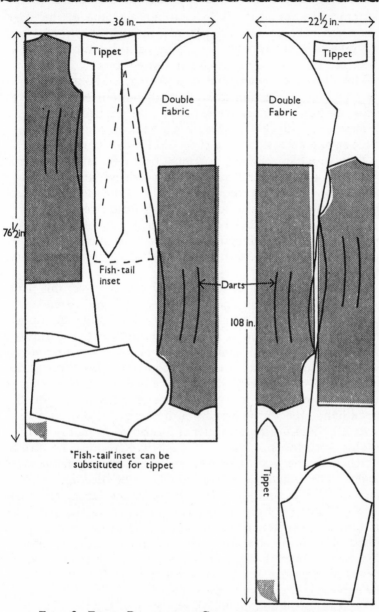

FIG. 26. FITTED PLANTAGENET GOWN, WITH AND WITHOUT
TIPPET
Left: Using 4¼ yards of 36 in. fabric; *Right:* Using 3 yards of 45 in. fabric

bottom edge rounded off to continue the line of the skirt. The train may, of course be longer, according to preference, but take care not to make it so long as to be unmanageable. Cut "fish tail" instead of tippet on dotted lines.

The sleeves are plain and close-fitting, without fullness at the shoulder, and trimmed with small buttons from elbow to wrist. Buttonholes are a waste of time, besides being a nuisance to fasten, and all that is needed is a 3 in. opening closed with three strong press studs or a short zip if funds permit.

To give added interest, a "tippet" may be added. This is cut as in diagram and tacked to the sleeve about midway between shoulder and elbow. Make tippet double, in contrasting colours; it can then be reversed for future use.

The neckline of this costume was a boat-shaped curve, plain or trimmed with contrasting braid, to match the girdle, worn round the hips, firmly anchored at centre back and at side seams.

Further variety can be achieved by wearing over this plain gown a sideless surcote, cut from piece (C) and extended as indicated in Fig. 27. (Back and front alike.) Like the tippet, this is detachable, and is a useful addition to the wardrobe. It is always shown in contemporary pictures as being edged with fur, which in some instances, comprises the whole of the upper part. Fur fabric, which now comes in such variety, is easier to handle and less cumbersome than real fur; on the other hand, the thrifty wardrobe mistress will always accept gratefully, and utilize, any gifts of fur, however moth-eaten!

This surcote is another adjunct which must be firmly attached to the main garment, to avoid making the wearer fidget. The fastenings can mostly be concealed in, or form part of, the trimmings. Add six or eight large, glittering buttons down the front of the basic dress and make matching buttonholes, which need not be works of art, since they will not show. Oversewn slits are quite adequate. Attach also at side seams, centre back, shoulder seams and back of neck, by means of large hooks and eyes—size 2 or 3. Sew the hook to the surcote and the eye to the dress.

Velvet is a suitable material, budget permitting, and about $4\frac{1}{2}$ yards of 36 in. material, used widthways, is a good average. If a train is required, cut as indicated in diagram. For greater

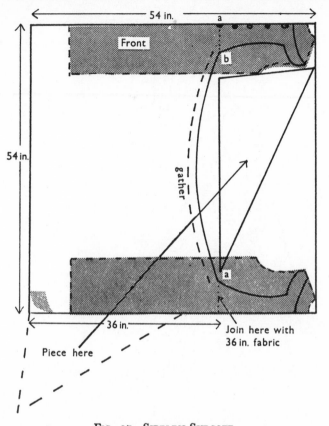

FIG. 27. SIDELESS SURCOTE
Using 4¼ yards of 36 in. fabric or 3 yards of 54 in. width

economy in cutting, the surcote can be cut in two sections, as
indicated by dotted line *a–b*.

Simple as these dresses are in the actual making, the cutting
needs especial care. Because there is no waist seam to allow
of juggling, you get no second chance—you must be right first
time. Darts and side seams allow a little leeway in the matter
of circumference, but the one vital measurement which *must*
be right is the neck to waist. As already mentioned, collected
statistics show that 75 per cent of English women are short-
waisted. Since many of the current patterns are of American
cut, it will mostly be found necessary to shorten by anything

FIG. 28. YORKIST GOWN WORN WITH STEEPLE HENNIN

up to 2 in. and this adjustment *must* be made before starting
to cut a dress with no waist seam, otherwise you will run into
trouble. Your safest course is to cut from the shift-line pattern,
without shaping at all. Then, at the first fitting, try the dress

inside out, and pin very carefully and evenly both side seams and darts. Double darts about 2 in. apart, either side of centre back and front, will give a closer fit. Tack firmly, and fit again, and only then trim away surplus on side seam. The final elegance of fit will be well worth the extra trouble.

Women also wore the houppelande, with the wide, dagged sleeve, and this is made in exactly the same way as the man's robe.

Dresses in the later Plantagenet period, *circa* Edward IV/ Richard III, show a marked upward movement of waist-line and a much fuller skirt. The predominant feature is the very wide, deep V-neck filled in with a contrasting gilet, which often matched the broad waist-band and underskirt. The neckline, cuffs and hem-line were frequently trimmed with fur, but velvet, brocade or dull satin may be substituted with equal effect.

Use pieces (*A*) and (*B*) of basic pattern, adapted (Fig. 29) as indicated by dotted lines. Do not cut the back lower than say 3 in. below the normal neck-line, otherwise the bodice will tend to slip off the shoulders. It is easier to superimpose the gilet, merely tacking it into place for future removal, the raw edges being concealed by the trimming. As in the earlier dresses, sleeves were plain and close fitting. Collar and cuffs, if not fur, will need interlining to give body, and the general effect will be enhanced if the contrasting hem-line trim is slightly padded with dressmakers wadding.

Depending upon the material used, there are two ways of cutting the skirt. If your material is stiff and heavy, use basic piece (*E*), adapted as in diagram. If a more voluminous skirt is preferred—and this does seem more in line with the prevalent style of the period—use a thinner, softer material, such as a fine rayon, Afgalaine, Jerseylaine or taffeta. Most of these materials come in 36 in. width, and as a fair average, you will need 7½ yards for the skirt. This allows for 6 widths each of 1¼ yards. Join at selvedges into one long strip; fold in half and pin raw edges evenly together; trim to curve as in top diagram and make back seam as indicated. Gather or form soft pleats as shown by dotted lines, and attach to bodice. This method of cutting gives considerable extra fullness without adding bulk round the waist, and it may be used for gowns of

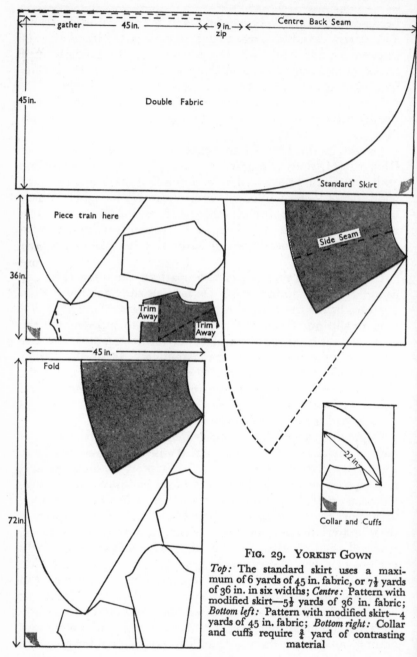

Centre Back Seam

gather — 45 in. — 9 in. zip

45 in.

Double Fabric

"Standard" Skirt

Piece train here

36 in.

Side Seam

Trim Away

Trim Away

45 in.

Fold

72 in.

~22 in.

Collar and Cuffs

FIG. 29. YORKIST GOWN

Top: The standard skirt uses a maximum of 6 yards of 45 in. fabric, or 7½ yards of 36 in. in six widths; *Centre:* Pattern with modified skirt—5½ yards of 36 in. fabric; *Bottom left:* Pattern with modified skirt—4 yards of 45 in. fabric; *Bottom right:* Collar and cuffs require ¾ yard of contrasting material

most periods. If the material you require is available in 45 in. width, 6 yards will be sufficient for the skirt, used width-ways.

HEADGEAR

Although there was a diversity of male headgear, it is usually found in practice that this is an unnecessary embarrass-ment. But if a hat *is* required, the "roundlet" is simple to make, and will serve for practically the whole of the Plantagenet era from Richard II onwards. Here again there is no need to

FIG. 30. ROUNDLET HAT

stick slavishly to actual historical accuracy. An effective imitation is a padded rouleau with a pleated valance. Make the rouleau from a *crossway* strip of material slightly longer than the actual head measurement. Join into a tube, and stuff fairly tightly with wadding or rolled latex foam such as is used for bath mats. Sew ends together to form circle. Cut valance as indicated in Fig. 31 and tack in large pleats to rouleau. The widest point should fall from the right, to cover the crown of the head, draping to the left.

A variety of caps can be contrived from old felt hats, and a study of the costume books will suggest an infinite range of ideas which are quite simple to put into practice.

Women's headgear was perhaps the most fantastic of any period in history—there was practically nothing they didn't try! The simplest was the steeple hennin—just a "dunce's cap," either pointed, with a floating veil attached to the tip, or truncated and worn with a stiffened butterfly veil or a

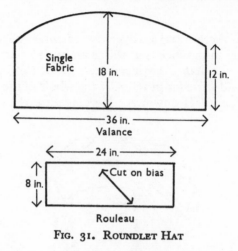

FIG. 31. ROUNDLET HAT

broad chin-band. Cut either of these from buckram, as in Fig. 33. Roll to form a cone, and join firmly with zig-zag stitches. Cover with material, either to match, or a contrast, and add an elastic to pass under the hair at the back. Sometimes worn with a broad stiffened band across forehead falling to shoulders, as in contemporary pictures. Strictly, no hair at all should be visible—even the nape and forehead were shaved; but this is one of the least attractive features of the period, and makes for difficulty and discomfort, so is often ignored. Several other styles can much more easily be used to conceal the hair, while remaining becoming. One is the heart-shaped head-dress, which is almost a "tea-cosy." Cut two sections as in Fig. 33—the straight edges should correspond to the head measurement and must fit firmly. Pad and interline with buckram. Work criss-cross stitching to resemble quilting, or use narrow gold braid or ribbon to give the effect of net-work, and finish the round edge with a narrow rouleau made in the same way as the chaperon. Tack veil to front and to top of curve.

For a very simple head-dress, make a small rouleau as before, and wear tilted over the forehead, with a long scarf passed under

Fig. 32. *Top:* STEEPLE HENNIN; *Bottom left:* HEARTSHAPED
HENNIN; *Bottom right:* TRUNCATED HENNIN

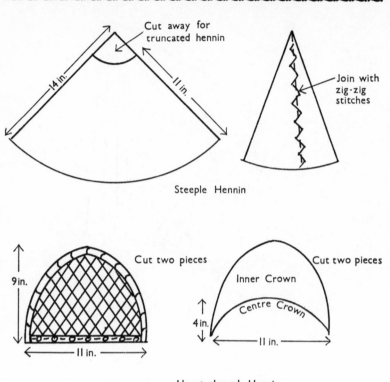

Cut away for truncated hennin

14 in.

11 in.

Join with zig-zig stitches

Steeple Hennin

9 in.

Cut two pieces

11 in.

Cut two pieces

Inner Crown

Centre Crown

4 in.

11 in.

Heart-shaped Hennin

FIG. 33. PATTERNS FOR HENNINS

the chin and through the centre of the rouleau, arranged in soft pleats falling to side and back. This is a most becoming head-dress for an older character, and may be worn with a gorget swathed round the throat.

The typical horned head-dress needs to be modified for comfort and manageability, and can be reduced to a pair of cones, about 7 in. high and 8½ in. at the base. A circle of buckram 7½ in. radius (15 in. diameter) cut into four pieces, will make two such head-dresses. Cover with material, and attach to a ½ in. elastic at the required angle. Make veil and gorget in soft material. The gorget is a straight piece of material up to, say, 18 in. wide and 1½ yards long. Arrange gorget under chin, passing under base of cones, and attach at crown of head to elastic band. Fasten veil to fall softly over

centre forehead, and at points of horns with hairgrips pushed
through veil and tip of cone. As a time-saving short cut, use
the cones which are supplied with the wool-winders for
Knitting Machines—about 1s. from Singers. These are not
generally in stock, but may be ordered if you are sufficiently
persistent!

Between Plantagenet and Tudor is an indeterminate period
which borrows much from the Italian Renaissance, and
provides a convenient set of styles for Shakespeare's non-
historical plays such as *Romeo and Juliet, The Merchant of Venice,
Much Ado about Nothing, The Taming of the Shrew*, etc. Considerable licence is permissible, provided it does not impinge too
definitely upon any precise era. For instance, the basic
houppelande style may be used, but the younger men might

FIG. 34. PUFFED SLEEVE

wear a very abbreviated version combined with the sleeve
shown in Fig. 34. This is one of the most useful and effective
sleeves in the wardrobe and I have used it in productions as
diverse as *Hamlet* and *The Cherry Orchard*, so it seems worth
while to describe it in detail, since it never seems to look out
of place. (It has just reappeared in the current pattern books!)
The sleeve is cut in two pieces, and must be mounted on a
lining, otherwise it will not puff properly. According to the
period, the lower sleeve may vary from elbow to armpit—the
latter more appropriate to women's "Regency" dresses.

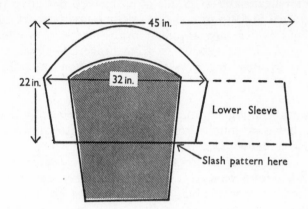

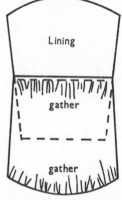

FIG. 35. PUFFED SLEEVE

Slash paper pattern across, and cut lower sleeve plain, with no alteration. Cut upper sleeve double the original width and depth, and interline with stiffening. If the appearance of slashing is required, apply this by machining vertical stripes in contrasting fabric. (If you have a swing-needle machine, simply zig-zag them on, but otherwise, turn under a single hem and top-stitch.) Place lining flat on table, and tack lower sleeve on it, right side up. By means of a double row of gathering, or by small, evenly spaced pleats, reduce lower edge of upper sleeve to the same measurement as upper edge of lower sleeve (Fig. 35). Now tack gathered edge to upper edge of lower

section. Machine both sections to lining. Gather or pleat top
of puff, and tack to sleeve head. Attach sleeve to garment
before finishing side seam, as previously advised, and after
final fitting, machine side and underarm seams in one operation, taking in the surplus of puff with the lining.

The same sleeve, with the puff reduced and not stiffened,
is suitable for incorporation with a long houppelande, or with
the puff stiffened and exaggerated, can be used for the women
as well.

Hennins can be discarded in favour of "Juliet" caps or even
little matching "pork pie" hats, and hair styles may be simple
and natural. This seeming hot-potch of fashion can be most
effective if carefully chosen, and selective borrowing can often
lift a production out of the rut.

Two further items in the wardrobe fall into this unidentified
period, and both form useful, economical and effective costumes for a number of minor characters for whom the wardrobe fund can never really afford much expenditure of either
money or time—serving men, pages and the like.

The first of these is a magyar tunic, but instead of joining the
shoulder seam, bind these edges, and the sleeve edges, with a
$\frac{1}{2}$ in. contrast. Cut a V-neck, bind this to match, and catch
together back and front at shoulder and arm-hole, similar to a
Greek chiton. Worn belted over a white cricket shirt, this is
one of the cheapest costumes to make—2 yards of 36 in.
material and a pair of tights, and a retainer is provided with a
smart livery.

The second "cheapie" is also worn over a cricket shirt.
The surcote which came into fashion in John's reign, developed
into the tabard, and in addition to being a useful item in its
own right, it can, if made up in bright colours, supply a very
smart outfit for a young page. Using just the back and front
of the basic pattern, cut the tabard with only very slight
extra fullness—a hand-span from a point halfway between
knees and hips, and finger-tip length (Fig. 36). Line and
interline—two or three thicknesses of newspaper give enough
body to preserve the line. Quilt interlining to lining to prevent
shifting and crumpling, and handle carefully to avoid creasing.
Join right shoulder-seam of lining; join right shoulder-seam
of tabard, and press open both seams. Snip carefully on neck

and arm-hole curves, and press inwards the ⅝ in. turning allowances all round, on both lining and tabard. Spread tabard flat on table and lay lining in place on top, wrong sides

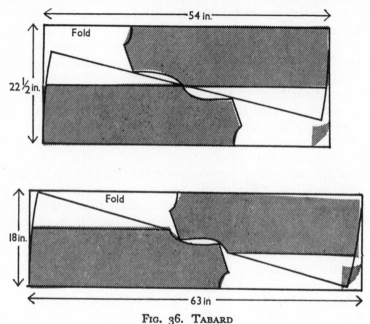

FIG. 36. TABARD

Above: Using 1¼ yards of 45 in. fabric; *Below:* Using 1¾ yards of 36 in. fabric

together. Tack together, then machine ¼ in. (or width of presser-foot) from the edge all the way round. Sew together at right under-arm; fasten on left shoulder and under-arm with *large* press-studs (furnishing size, about ½ in. diameter).

The functional use of the tabard proper was originally to protect armour from rust, and later to display the wearer's blazon. The basic method of making is the same, but the material will need to be stronger, such as sail-cloth, denim or canvas; the devices can be painted on, or cut out of felt, etc., and stuck on.

CHAPTER THREE

TUDOR

THE change from Plantagenet to Tudor was drastic, but no fundamental difficulty of actual cutting emerges, and all that is necessary is ingenuity in the matter of decoration.

The white shirt dates from this period. It does not always need to be a separate garment, however, but can be simulated by a fill-in at the neck, and an appliqué "slash" on the tunic sleeve.

FIG. 37. TUDOR MAN

A typical costume of the period would consist of a square-necked tunic or doublet, knee-length, belted, and with plain sleeves, over which would be worn a loose gown, cut slightly longer, with wider sleeves similar to those already described in

FIG. 38. FLARED JERKIN WITH PUFFED SLEEVES

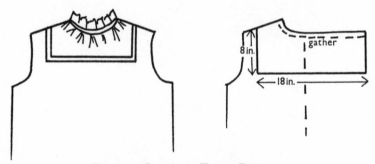

FIG. 39. GILET FOR TUDOR DOUBLET

the chapter on Norman costume. The gown is open down the front, with a broad facing of fur extending into a wide, square collar. Cut the tunic as in Fig. 4, with a square neck, 6 in. or 7 in. deep in the front, but only about 2 in. wider at the shoulder; it is not necessary to square off the back neckline. The white "gilet" is cut from the top of the basic pattern, as in Fig. 39. Gather the lower edge and attach to tunic; gather at neck and finish with a bias binding. Alternatively, face with bias to form a casing, and run a draw-string of fine cotton cord.

In the later Tudor styles, the doublet was shortened to knee-length, with the skirt considerably fuller, making it necessary

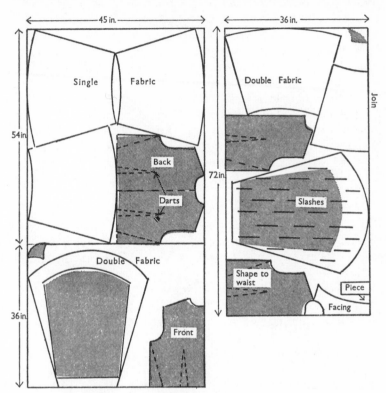

FIG. 40. TUDOR DOUBLET WITH FULL SKIRT
Left: Using 3½ yards of 45 in. fabric; *Right:* Using 4 yards of 36 in. fabric

to cut the garment with a waist seam. A much closer fit is essential, and it is therefore better to cut a newspaper pattern of the upper section, using pieces (*A*) and (*B*) of Fig. 1, modified as shown in Fig. 40. For the skirt section, use piece (*E*) of Fig. 2, wider and shorter, as indicated on diagram.

Sleeves were large, and padded, with the shirt pulled through the slashings. Use piece (*D*), Fig. 1, modified as in Fig. 40; cut also an interlining of wadding and an inner lining, all the same size. Sandwich wadding between sleeve and lining, and quilt together with long tacks on the inside. Before joining to main garment, add slashings, which should be vertical and regular. They are best made from fine white

3

lawn—old handkerchiefs come in useful. Cut a strip about 4 in. wide, turn in and hem long edges, then divide into 6 in. lengths. (1 yard of lawn, lingerie rayon or nylon, will make 54 slashings.) Turn down raw short edges and run a double gathering thread, drawing together tightly. Stitch to sleeve at regular intervals—it is unnecessary to sew down the long edges, but a couple of tacks at the half-way point will keep them from going "stringy." Finish sleeve at wrist with a narrow pleated frill about 2 in. wide. Join sleeve to garment as described in previous chapter on Plantagenet. Finish doublet with a narrow frill at the neck, and fasten down the front as far as the waist with hooks and eyes, or a concealed open-ended zip.

A jerkin is worn over the doublet, and this may be either sleeveless, or have half, puffed sleeves, or hanging sleeves, similar to those worn with the houppelande. For the puffed sleeve, follow the instructions already given at the end of Chapter Two, omitting the lower sleeve. The hanging sleeve has already been described in the same chapter, and merely requires to be made shorter (to the hem of doublet or jerkin), with the opening suitably enlarged to accommodate the padded sleeve.

The body of the jerkin is similar in cut to the houppelande, but should be fuller. Fig. 41 shows how to cut this, using pieces (A) and (B) of basic pattern. Trim with a wide tuxedo facing, with a broad, square collar. (Considerable exaggeration is permissible in this period—Henry VIII was practically square in outline.)

Velvet is the most suitable material for the jerkin, and the best value will be found in the soft furnishing department. It is a counsel of perfection that velvet should be made up with the pile all running the same way, but this makes for very extravagant cutting, and is not really necessary, since lighting and movement will not give the audience time to notice the difference.

It is, in fact, easier to cut single material, but be careful to turn the pattern over before cutting the second piece. Alternatively, cut one piece, then place this over the main length, wrong sides together. Pin at about 4 in. intervals and cut an identical piece. Tack seams firmly before machining, as

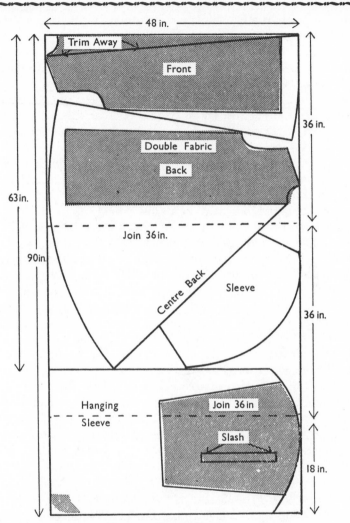

FIG. 41. TUDOR JERKIN
Using 7 yards of 36 in. fabric (5½ yards without hanging sleeve), or
5 yards of 48 in. cloth (3¼ yards without hanging sleeve)

velvet "creeps" under the pressure of the machine foot, and on a long seam can end up as much as 2 in. out, with one side badly puckered.

The jerkin should be lined with a bright contrasting satin or taffeta, and this is an instance where the lining must be made up separately; allow jerkin to hang for a couple of days, to "drop," before inserting the lining. Take up a 3 in. hem on the jerkin, and slip-stitch the lining carefully to avoid any drag. It is better to stitch about 2½ in. from the bottom edge, allowing the surplus to fall downwards in a loose pleat.

The humbler characters—citizens, retainers, etc.—may wear a jerkin of more fustian material, such as furnishing rep or serge, in fairly subdued colours, trimmed with a toning contrast. The more substantial citizens, merchants, burgesses and so on, would still wear fur. The enormous puffed sleeves should be omitted, and the sleeve at Fig. 35 is suitable— attached to the doublet as instructed in Chapter Two. A white frill at the wrist indicates the under-shirt.

Later still in the Tudor period the skirts of the doublet were worn considerably shorter, being no more than, in dress-making parlance, a peplum, under which puffed trunk-hose are worn. These are exaggerated bloomers, and can be cut from the short pyjama-trouser pattern, doubled in width. In some portraits they are shown plain, in others they are "paned" and gathered into a band. In most productions, however, it is sufficient to make them with an elastic top and bottom. More detailed instructions are given in the next chapter, as this style, with variations, lasted up till Stuart times.

Many of the portraits of the period show the doublet unfastened to the waist, permitting the shirt to be seen—white, with lace at the wrist, and often exquisitely embroidered. This, of course, is not often possible, but as shirts are also one of the stable assets of the wardrobe, it is worth while to select, say, broderie anglaise for the front panel and sleeve ends.

Men in Tudor times seem to have been very cap-minded, particularly the older generation, who wore a square cap, shown in Fig. 43. This may also have an additional flap at the back.

Cut four pieces as indicated in diagram. If made from black felt, an inter-lining is unnecessary, but velvet, which was frequently used, will need an interlining and a silk lining. Join interlining and cap all in one operation, make silk lining separately, turn inwards ⅝ in. at lower edge, and slip-stitch lining by hand. It is simpler to join the quarters two-and-two, then join the two half-sections together.

FIG. 42. TUDOR CAPS
Top left and right: Square caps; *Bottom left:* Henry VIII cap;
Bottom right: Bonnet

Hats can be made from felt—old trilbies cut down in the crown can be used, or the same effect can be obtained by attaching a round felt brim to a beret. The brim is then squared off, giving the characteristic line shown, for instance, in the portrait of Henry VII. It seems to have been a matter of personal taste as to whether or not the point was worn centre front—the portraits of the time show both styles.

If a felt hat is used, turn up the brim and pinch at four equidistant points, which can be rounded inwards and the "pinch" kept in place by a couple of buttons, or tied with a thong.

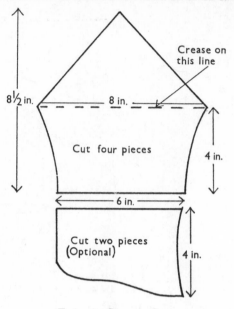

FIG. 43. SQUARE CAP

It is worth while to make and keep a pattern for the felt brim, since this can also be used to make the velvet hats like tam-o'-shanters of the later Tudor and Elizabethan eras. Fold a single sheet of newspaper in half. Using a radius equal to $\frac{1}{6}$th of head measurement $+ \frac{1}{2}$ in., mark out a half-circle. Now describe a further concentric circle with a radius increased by the required width of the brim, as shown in Fig. 44.

EXAMPLE: Head measurement $= 21$ in. $\div 6 = 3\frac{1}{2}$ in.
Radius of inner circle therefore $= 3\frac{1}{2}$ in. $+ \frac{1}{2}$ in.
$= 4$ in.
Radius of outer circle therefore $= 4$ in. $+ 3$ in.
(brim) $= 7$ in.

This will give a flat circle about 3 in. larger than is required. Reduce to correct size by cutting away a 3 in. segment, as indicated on diagram. This will eliminate the surplus fullness of the circular brim. For more economical cutting, divide pattern into four pieces and place on felt as shown in diagram. Join into circle by a $\frac{1}{8}$ in. seam—this will give the required

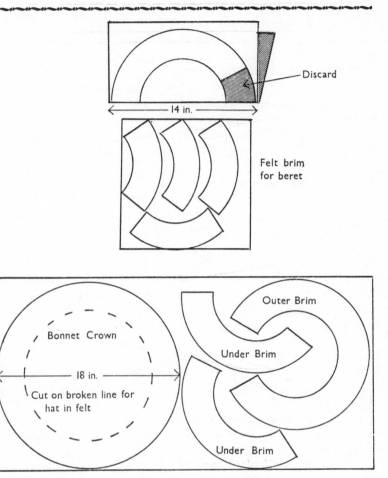

FIG. 44. TUDOR CAP AND BONNET

squared-off effect. Stretch slightly, or trim carefully, to fit head measurement, and stitch firmly over band of beret.

In the later Tudor period, the same type of cap as already described was still worn, and for the humbler characters the "felt-and-beret" combination will serve. But for Henry VIII himself, and his courtiers, something more elaborate is necessary. Black velvet was generally used, embellished with jewels and ostrich feathers or swansdown, both of which can be obtained quite reasonably from theatrical suppliers—for a list of these see Appendix. The contemporary Tudor paintings in art galleries and the great houses now open to the public make further description superfluous.

The pattern for the brim has already been described. Make two circles of velvet—all in one piece if material is available, or in four sections, in which case allow a ⅝ in. turning on each short edge, as well as on curved edges. Cut a stiff interfacing from either buckram, esparterie, or layers of brown paper, depending on the degree of durability required. *Do not allow turnings on curved edges of stiffening.* Make flat joins on short edges and stitch firmly, either with wide zig-zag tacks, or with two rows of machine stitching at least ½ in. apart.

With right sides together, machine together the outer edges of the upper and under brim; carefully notch turnings all round so that they will lie flat, flatten seam with thumb-nail (velvet must never be ironed as this marks it and flattens the pile), and turn right side out. Sandwich the stiffening between the upper and lower brim, pushing the outer edge firmly to the machine stitching. Anchor with dabs of Copydex, and tack into place with large V-tacks. Draw under-brim taut over stiffening, pin into place, matching raw edges, and machine together, wrong sides together, ⅝ in. from edge.

The crown of this cap is a circle of velvet, with a diameter equal to that of the brim, plus 6 in. (or twice width of brim). An average measurement for an adult is 18 in. across. Cut a circle of non-woven interlining—not buckram or esparterie as this will not gather. Tack interlining to velvet, and gather on to brim; it is easier to reduce to size by means of pinch-pleats at 1 in. intervals; a gathering thread always breaks at the wrong moment, and the even spacing of gathers can be difficult.

Machine crown to brim—two rows of stitching are advisable, for extra strength, since there is often much doffing and donning of hats; snip edges of brim carefully, and turn all raw edges inwards to crown. Cut a silk lining the same size as crown, turn in raw edge, gather and slip-stitch into place over raw edges of velvet crown and brim.

The king would wear his cap with the brim turned up all round, the plume or swansdown curling over the edge, and the whole brim studded with jewels. Alternatively, one side might be caught up with a single jewel, which held the plume in place.

A variant of this cap, worn by younger men, omitted the brim altogether; a circle of black velvet, slightly smaller in diameter, is gathered into a plain head-band. This cap also is jewelled and a small plume added.

Another Tudor cap consists of the same brim, joined at the inner edge to an identical piece which now forms the under-crown, the upper crown being a circle about 14 in. diameter, interlined. To assemble, first make the brim as previously described. Next, sandwich the brim between under-crown and under-crown *lining* and machine with a double row of stitching. Snip curved edges, draw the lining and under-crown level, and tack the edges. Attach the upper crown, easing in any extra fullness. Turn raw edges inwards, and slip-stitch the upper-crown lining over these edges.

All the foregoing may appear to be much ado about caps, but as with cloaks, they are useful permanent items of the wardrobe, and being mostly black, will fit into any colour schemes in a wide range of productions. The extra work involved will, in the long run, save time and expense.

Gloves now come into the picture, and may be embroidered and jewelled; if there is a glove-maker in the house, press-gang her into making gloves of leather, chamois-leather or felt. If not, add embroidered gauntlets of felt, chamois or glove leather, cut from the cuff pattern in Fig. 1, and attach to bought gloves.

Women's dresses carried over into the early Tudor period a few of the characteristics of the later Plantagenet–Yorkist era, notably the wide sleeves and fur-banded skirts, caught up to show an underskirt of some other rich material. The waist-line dropped to its natural position, and the wide V-neck gave way to a square neckline, trimmed with fur or velvet and filled in with a white lawn "gilet" to represent the chemise under-garment. The instructions given in the previous chapter can therefore apply to the early Tudor gowns, and a study of portraits and books on the subject will indicate the characteristic modifications necessary. The long hanging sleeve as shown in Fig. 20 is trimmed with a deep band of fur to match the skirt, and the plain under-sleeve matches the underskirt. The

FIG. 45. TUDOR WOMAN

latter need be no more than a deep flounce of velvet or satin, mounted on a calico petticoat from stock. Alternatively, instead of the hanging sleeve, a plain, close-fitting sleeve matching the over-gown can be trimmed with a broad fur cuff. A portrait of Elizabeth of York (queen to Henry VII) painted by Holbein the Elder depicts her in a gown of this style, trimmed with ermine; this can be simulated by using white brushed rayon or fur-fabric, embroidered with black Angora wool "tails."

Later, the silhouette changed to the bell-shaped line which lasted right through to the reign of Elizabeth I.

The bodice remained close fitting, with a wide, square neckline extending to the arm-hole. Cut the back of the bodice high enough to carry the sleeve, otherwise it becomes impossible to keep the sleeves from slipping off the shoulders.

Use pieces (A) and (B) of the basic pattern (Fig. 2), modified

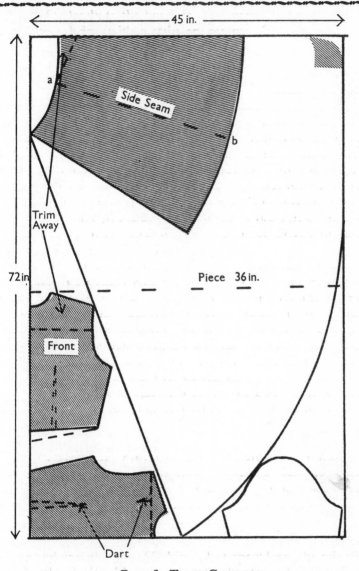

45 in.

72 in

a

Side Seam

b

Trim
Away

Piece 36 in.

Front

Dart

FIG. 46. TUDOR GOWN
Using 4 yards of 45 in. or 5 yards of 36 in. fabric (plus hanging sleeve
shown in Fig. 48)

as indicated in Fig. 46. The front may either have a slight
downward curve, or be brought to a point.

The bell-shaped skirt is left open from waist to hem, to show the contrasting underskirt, and the underskirt can be simulated by an inset front panel, or, the whole front as far as the side seams may be made of contrasting material, which should match the under-sleeve.

The outer skirt is cut from piece (*E*) of the basic pattern, Fig. 2, modified as in diagram, Fig. 46. The pattern lay-out depends upon the material chosen. It is most economical to

FIG. 47. KATHARINE HOWARD SLEEVE

use material with no design at all, or with a design which has no definite direction; a design with a defined "stripe" or medallion, with no up-and-down, is still a reasonable proposition; a design with a very noticeable up-and-down is extravagant, and not really worth considering, because there is such an attractive and extensive range without this disadvantage. Furnishing brocades up to 108 in. wide are available in most department stores, at comparatively reasonable prices; these have the requisite "body" and richness of colour, and are a delight to any wardrobe mistress.

If the material used is stiff and thick, the pattern must be adjusted first to fit the individual waist measurement, so that it can be attached to the bodice without pleats or gathers. Cut away as indicated by broken line, to allow for dropped curve

or pointed bodice. If the underskirt is to be an inset piece, cut
a triangle having a base line of about 27 in., with sides equal to
the length of the main skirt (Fig. 48).

Sleeves can be reduced to three basic pieces; a close-fitting
upper sleeve, varying from elbow length to a cap-sleeve with
hardly any underarm seam: a voluminous hanging sleeve,
deep enough to be turned back to show a rich, contrasting
lining: a puffed under-sleeve, sometimes slashed to show
the white chemise sleeve, and finished with a white lawn
frill.

For the upper sleeve, which should match the body of the
gown, use piece (F) of the basic pattern, shortened as required.
The hanging sleeve is cut in the same way as was shown in
Fig. 15, suitably enlarged as in Fig. 48; the method of assembly
is the same as given in Chapter One. The under-sleeve need
only be a "sham" to the elbow, cut as in Fig. 48.

Assemble gown in the following order—

Sandwich between sleeve and sleeve lining the back bodice
(from shoulder to under-arm), and the small under-arm portion of the front bodice. Tack all round the head of the sleeve.
To prevent the front of the sleeve-head stretching, machine
over $\frac{1}{2}$ in. tape, and leave a 24 in. length of tape from underarm
at the point where neckline and sleeve meet, to tie centre back
before zipping up. This will stop the wide neck-line from
gaping.

Tack the side seam of the bodice and the underarm seam of
the upper sleeve, and fit carefully at this stage. The bodice
must be as tight as is consistent with comfort, and if you are
coping with a full-busted wench, the only way to get the top of
the bodice to fit properly is to make small darts—one centre
front and two each side over the bust.

Make the lower hanging sleeve by the same method as
described in Chapter One, and attach to the upper sleeve in the
same way. If fur-lined, make up by hand and sew fabric sleeve
to fur at outer edge and at armhole.

Join underskirt triangle to centre front of skirt. If, however,
the underskirt is to extend to the side seam, cut as indicated
by broken line a–b (centre front to fold). Make a 3 in. hem
down each front, which will hang free, and machine underskirt to main skirt along the line a–b. (There will be no actual

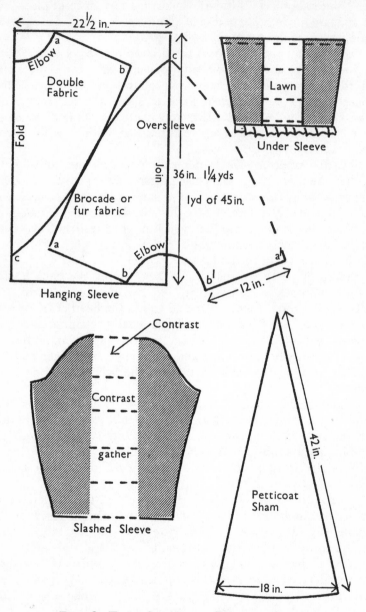

FIG. 48. TUDOR SLEEVES AND PETTICOAT SHAM

side seam since each side of the skirt is cut in one piece, but this is the point at which it should meet the side seam of the bodice. The whole skirt can in fact be cut as one piece.)

It is easier to join the skirt at the waist before joining the back seam, and this should now be done. Then join back seam of skirt, leaving open 8 in. below the waist. Insert zip centre back.

Later, in the reigns of Edward VI and Mary I, the styles remained basically the same, but with a variation possibly due to Mary's austere modesty, in that the neckline was entirely filled in, either with embroidered gauze or muslin, or the bodice was cut high to the neck, and a graceful, stand-up white collar added. Make this of white lawn (double), or of the same material as the gown, lined with white satin, using the "arum lily" pattern in Fig. 23. The front corners may be sharpened and extended to taste. Wire the edge, and curve to shape.

A further sleeve modification which goes well with this collar is also shown in Fig. 48. The hanging cuff and false under-sleeve are discarded, and a plain sleeve, slashed from shoulder to wrist, is both economical and effective. Use piece (F) of the basic pattern, cut down the centre, and insert a contrasting strip of material 6 in. wide. Taffeta, silk, linen or lawn are all suitable. Gather at intervals as indicated in diagram, and finish with a knot of ribbon or a jewel. One of the portraits of poor Katharine Howard depicts this style, and the play which immediately comes to mind is *The Rose without a Thorn*. The illustrations in Doreen Yarwood's *English Costume* provide end-less inspiration, and I have found it extremely difficult to be selective. But in one's early days as wardrobe mistress, simpli-city is safer, and the wilder extravagances of design can be left until you have gained experience.

Throughout the whole Tudor period up to the reign of Elizabeth I, two head-dresses persisted—the gable, and the French hood. The former does not need to be the intricate contraption depicted in contemporary portraits. The latter is one of the easiest and most becoming head-dresses in the ward-robe.

The earliest form of the gable, as seen in tne pictures of Elizabeth of York, queen of Henry VII, is more sharply

FIG. 49. TUDOR HEAD-DRESSES

Top left: Gable Head-dress, Elizabeth of York; *Top right:* Gable Head-dress, Katharine of Aragon· *Bottom:* French Hood

pointed and not quite so wide as that worn by later queens—Katharine of Aragon, Jane Seymour and Katharine Parr, but the basic principle is the same, as is the making of it.

The gable itself is a "roof" of buckram, about 12 in. × 6 in. Make creases at the centre, and about 5 in. either side, and cut the "barge-board" section as indicated in Fig. 50. (I can think of no other adequate term to describe this section; it is just like the fretted wood-work which finishes off the gables of

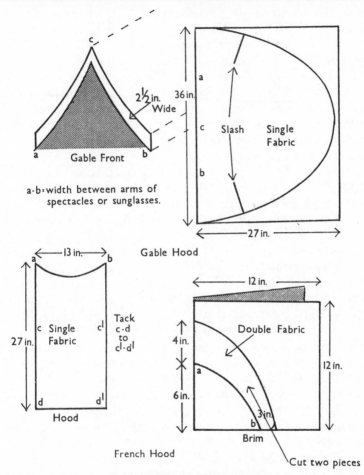

FIG. 50. TUDOR HEAD-DRESSES

houses.) Oversew this section to the "roof," and wire the seam and inner edge with either millinery wire or galvanized wire, which is easier to bend to shape.

The hood is black, and of light-weight material. A fine ring-velvet is suitable for the queen and her ladies, otherwise a soft satin or some other material which will fall in soft folds—taffeta is too stiff. Three-quarters of a yard of 36 in. fabric is sufficient.

Slash at centre front and gable-ends to a depth equal to

twice the width of the "barge-board." Tack from slash to slash, along top edge of "roof," and take the extra allowance over the edge of the "barge-board" to the inside. Copydex or sew into place, and continue this allowance down each side to form a hem, but without any interfacing. This will allow the veil to frame the face, whereas any stiffening gives a hard, box-like effect. Trim the "barge-board" and hem with pearl embroidery or pearled sequin strip; make a broad band of similar trimming over the top of the gable, falling to the shoulder, as in portraits.

Attach the "roof" firmly to a *broad* Alice Band (to prevent rocking), and slash at shoulder, as diagram.

The later gable headdress, as worn by Katharine of Aragon, etc., had a much wider angle, without the curved edge rising to a sharp point. This is consequently easier to make, as the "barge-board" need not be the awkwardly-curved separate piece described above. Cut the "roof" $2\frac{1}{2}$ in. wider, clip $2\frac{1}{2}$ in. at angles, and crease inwards, overlapping cut edge to make "barge-board," which is covered with a piece of striped silk (see portrait). An underhood of stiff white material—double organdie, starched lawn or calico, is necessary, since the pendants are tied back, thus showing this white coif. This is a straight strip of material long enough to reach nearly to the shoulders, and about 1 in. wider than the "roof." Mitre inwards at angles and make hem in the same way as previously described for the early Tudor gable. Stiffen the hem with ribbon-wire so that it will curve in slightly to the cheek; add pearl trimming as before. Attach to "roof," then stitch hood on top. Finally, add the jewelled "pendants" which are then looped back and fastened on the crown of the head, leaving the hood to drape down the back. Make the "pendants" as light as possible to avoid dragging.

The best foundation for the French hood is the crown of an old felt or (preferably) velour or melusine hat. Cut off the brim, and hollow out the back-neck so that the crown sits comfortably like a bonnet. Edge the front with a tiny flat frill of white lawn or gold organza. Stitch back the brim so that it turns back on to the crown, and reaches just to the ears. Cut away surplus. Trim both edges of brim with pearls or braid.

The hood is just a straight strip about 9 in. wide, hanging

down the back nearly to the waist. Cut one edge in a concave curve and stitch to crown just under brim.

Instead of using a hat, the cap may be a stiffened brim attached to an Alice band. Cut this as shown in Fig. 50, using buckram or esparterie, or even cardboard. Cover with matching material or black velvet. Cut one piece of material the same size as the buckram and paint the edges with clear nail-varnish to prevent fraying. Cut another piece, allowing $\frac{3}{8}$ in. turnings all round. Carefully clip all curved edges about $\frac{1}{2}$ in. inwards, at 1 in. intervals. Lay the material face downwards and fit the buckram on top (a dab of Copydex here and there will prevent shifting). Copydex the edges all round, and fold inwards, over the edge of the buckram, pressing down firmly. Copydex the smaller piece over the stuck-down edges. The hood should then be a strip of material of the same length as before, but slightly wider, 12–13 in. Stitch to the bandeau, catching the edges inwards from the back of the neck downwards. The hood may also have strings tied under the chin, particularly if worn by older characters.

NOTE: All these gowns of the later Tudor period should be worn over a hooped petticoat, for which instructions are given in a later chapter.

CHAPTER FOUR

ELIZABETHAN

ELIZABETH I inherited her father's love of finery, and it is essential that costume for this period should have as much ornamentation as can be contrived. The basic line, however, follows on from the previous period, merely becoming more and more exaggerated.

The doublet was close-fitting, pointed in front, and the depth of the peplum varied considerably. Cut the doublet from the basic pattern modified as in Fig. 53. Trim with braid or applied slashings, and interline the front for extra

FIG. 51. ELIZABETHAN MAN

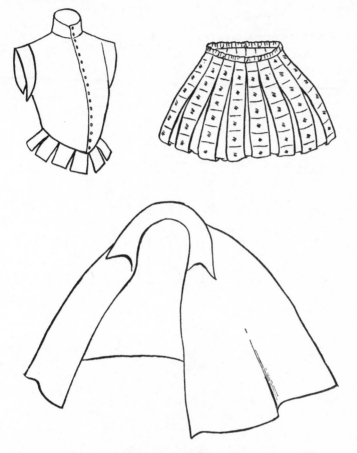

FIG. 52. *Top left:* DOUBLET; *Top right:* TRUNK HOSE; *Bottom:*
SHORT FLARED CLOAK

"body." Cut the peplum as in diagram. Use the plain sleeve
pattern, trimmed to match doublet, and add a padded shoulder
roll. This must be cut on the cross, and stuffed with wadding
or backed with foam rubber. It is easier to make this roll
separately and attach to the finished doublet.

The predominant style of neck-wear was the ruff, which can
vary considerably in size. Use starched lawn, organdie or
tarlatan, cut into strips and pleated evenly into 2 in. pleats.

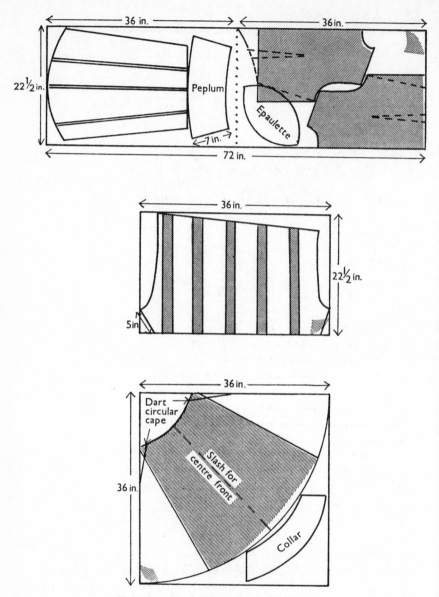

FIG. 53. *Top:* ELIZABETHAN DOUBLET
Using 2½ yards of 36 in. cloth or 2 yards of 45 in. cloth
Centre: TRUNK HOSE, PANED OR SLASHED
Using 1¼ yards of 36 in. or 1 yard of 45 in. cloth
Bottom: SHORT FLARED CAPE WITH COLLAR
Using 1 yard of 36 in. cloth for plain cape, or 2 yards of 36 in. cloth for
circular cape

Pierce the inner edges top and bottom and thread with elastic. (One elastic is not sufficient, as the ruff will twist.) The amount of material required will vary according to the neck measurement; one yard of 36 in. tarlatan will cut into 18 strips 2 in. wide or 12 strips 3 in. wide, and will pleat down to about 1 in., so 1 yard will make an average-size ruff. Remember that the deeper the ruff, the more strips will be required, and for a very deep cart-wheel ruff, oversew the inner edge of each pleat to the one before, to get rid of the fullness.

An alternative neck finish, made familiar by the Shakespeare portraits, is the plain "whisk" collar, cut from the pyjama collar, without the sharp point. Tie at the neck with fine cord.

The trunk hose were simply very wide, short "bloomers." Cut them from the pyjama trouser pattern, extended in width, and shortened, Fig. 53. Interline, and tack these two pieces together first; the paned effect is achieved by applied contrasting strips. If the trunks are made from soft material, they can be lined with calico, with an extra line of machine stitching top and bottom to form a casing through which strong elastic is threaded. Thicker material such as furnishing brocade, should be mounted on a close-fitting lining. Pleat fullness to fit leg, machine lining to trunks, right sides together, turn right side out and pleat again at waist, leaving an opening centre back.

Mount on petersham and finish with large hooks and eyes —the slit will disappear in the fullness.

This costume can be made all in one by joining the trunks at the waist, under the peplum. Insert long zip centre back.

Instead of the jerkin, short cloaks were worn. Use the flared skirt pattern and cut as in Fig. 53. If a fuller cloak is required, cut two pieces; slash one diagonally, and join on the straight edges. This preserves the bias-cut centre back and avoids an ugly side droop. Cut collar from the pyjama collar pattern and interline. Line cloak with a bright contrast.

To make up, join side seams of lining and of cloak (for the fuller cloak); place lining over the cloak, right sides together, and machine down right front, round curved lower edge and up left front. Turn right side out and press. Make up collar in the same way, and machine to cloak but *not* to cloak lining.

FIG. 54. ELIZABETHAN WOMAN

Press turnings downwards and slip-stitch lining over raw edges.
Finish off with silk cords and tassels.

Hats can be made in the same way as the Tudor "bonnet,"
but with smaller brims. Felt or velour hats can also be re-
blocked and trimmed with jewels and plumes.

Shoes should be as plain and unobtrusive as possible, though
they may be trimmed with bows for the more dandified
characters.

The essential line of women's costumes also followed on from
the early Tudor. Cutting and making are the same; the
variations lie in neckline and sleeves. The former incorporates
the ruff, made in the same way as described above, and edged
with lace.

Sleeves were puffed and slashed, and became progressively
larger, being held out with stiffening. Cut from basic piece
(F) as modified in Fig. 55 and finish with a padded roll.

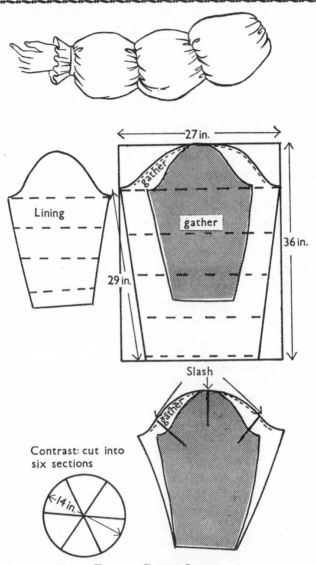

FIG. 55. PUFFED SLEEVES
Top: Typical Elizabethan sleeve; *Centre and Bottom:* Patterns

An effective variation of this sleeve is to make three downward slashes about 8 in. deep, as indicated on diagram, and
insert contrasting pieces. Cut a complete circle of the contrast,

using a radius $\frac{1}{2}$ in. less than the slash, and divide into six equal "slices." Turn under a $\frac{1}{4}$ in. seam allowance on each slash, tapering to nothing at point, and lap over straight edges of insert. Top-stitch close to edge and, if the material frays, paint raw edges with colourless nail varnish. (Overstitch if using a swing-needle machine.) Run a double gathering thread round sleeve head and draw up to fit armhole.

The puffed sleeve is mounted on a lining cut from the plain sleeve pattern. Cut taffeta sleeve as in Fig. 55 and mark guide lines on sleeve and on lining as indicated. Run double gathering threads across taffeta sleeve, and draw up to fit lining. Machine to lining on the four marked lines, and trim with jewels. Add a small lace ruffle at wrist. Insert sleeve into armhole, and pleat in the puffs on the underarm seam. An elaboration of this style is to make the outer sleeve entirely of ribbon loops. Mark out the lining in the same way and stitch lengths of ribbon, allowing about $1\frac{1}{2}$ times the length of the sleeve.

Skirts, until about 1575, continued as in the previous reigns, and were still worn open, displaying the rich underskirt. Then a padded hip roll was added, and the top of the skirt was gathered at the waist. Use the standard skirt at Fig. 29, but make allowance for the amount of "take-up."

The wheel farthingale came in about 1590. This made a considerable change in the silhouette, giving a "dressing-table" line, and a frill was added to the bodice; this is a straight piece of matching fabric, about 3 yards long, wide enough to reach to the edge of the farthingale, but narrowed slightly at each end because the "hub" of the wheel is positioned nearer to the front edge.

A wheel of about 63 in. is a practical average size, and a change in the cut of the skirt is necessary. To avoid bulky gathers at the waist, it is cut in two sections. The top section is a strip of material 64 in. long, and 9 in. wide, graduated to 4 in. each end, Fig. 56. This corresponds to the size of the hoop, the narrowest part being centre front. Try on hoop, instructions for which are given in Chapter Ten, and measure from edge to floor in a straight line—this skirt hangs straight, not bell-shaped. Cut a 4-yard or 5-yard strip to the required depth, and pleat on to the upper section by the method outlined in Chapter Ten. More pleats will be needed than for the petticoat, but

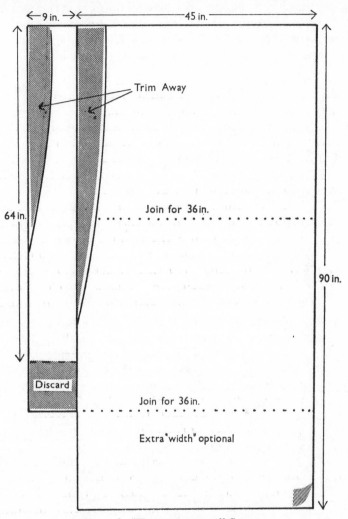

FIG. 56. "DRESSING-TABLE" SKIRT
Using 7¼ yards of 36 in. cloth (maximum) or 6 yards of 45 in. (maximum)

the fullness is distributed evenly all round the hoop. This skirt does not trail, and may even be instep length, since the fashion was for very much shorter skirts than hitherto.

The ruff also changed, and was worn open in the front, with a low, square neckline, similar to the Tudor style. Add a small triangular piece from shoulder to armhole (Fig. 57), and fasten down open edges of ruffle, which will need supports at the back. Take two 18 in. lengths of 20-gauge galvanized wire and cover with tape or sticking plaster. Bend back ½ in. each end and pad

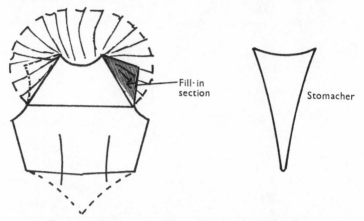

FIG. 57. BODICE WITH OPEN RUFF AND STOMACHER

to prevent scratching. Sew about 5 in. each end down armhole seam and centre back, forming two supporting hoops of wire which will hold the ruffle in position. *NOTE:* if bodice has a centre back fastening, the ruffle must either be in two sections, sewn to bodice and pinned together centre back with small safety pins, or else made all in one and pinned or press-studded round neck of bodice.

A further embellishment was a winged gauze collar and floating veil. Make the wings of two large semi-circles of gauze, net or lace, cut double. Join on curved edges, insert the wire and tack in place, leaving 5 in. tails each end. Trim edges with beads, jewels, pearls or galloon; gather each lower edge to fit across shoulders, and attach to dress, sewing down the wire tails as before. (This also helps to support the ruff.) Take a straight length of similar gauze, etc., gather to fit across the shoulders, machine to thin tape, and fasten to gown with tiny safety-pins. Any portrayal of Mary Queen of Scots would need this veil, as well as the small heart-shaped cap. Cut this from a half-circle of fine lawn or organdie, 24 in. diameter. Gather the straight edge tight, wire the curved edge and bend it into wings as in the portraits (Fig. 58). Edge with narrow lace.

The standing lace collar is also wired in the same way, but is brought to the front and fastened to the point where armhole and neckline meet. A further support is necessary at centre back.

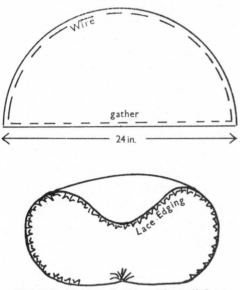

FIG. 58. "MARY QUEEN OF SCOTS" CAP

The stomacher is an inverted triangle about 9 in. wide and 15 in. deep. As it is stiffened with buckram, it should not be made so deep as to buckle when the wearer sits down. It is made separately, and can be of richer material than the basic gown, and embellished with jewels or (in later Stuart costume) with bows.

Cut the buckram to the required size, and cut a similar piece of fabric, allowing ⅝ in. turnings all round. Cut lining, also allowing ⅝ in. turnings. Place material face downwards, position buckram, and Copydex turnings inwards on to buckram, snipping where necessary (the top edge of the stomacher can be curved). Turn in seam allowance on lining, press, pin over raw edges and slip-stitch into place.

Fasten to gown with strong press-studs. This can be used as

FIG. 59. ELIZABETHAN WOMAN, *circa* 1600

an addition to the basic costume to add variety in production. As an alternative, sew hooks to the bodice front of a coat-style dress, and work strong loops down each side of the stomacher. This method is preferable for the Stuart costumes (see Chapter Five).

Most of these dresses are easier to get into if made coat-wise and fastened at the centre front. The necessary small placket slit will be concealed by the point of the stomacher.

CHAPTER FIVE

STUART AND PURITAN

No very drastic changes appeared at first with the new dynasty, and the same basic methods of cutting may still be employed, at least for the reign of James I, which is largely transitional.

The jerkin/doublet remained, with plain sleeves, padded epaulettes, and peplums of varying depths, which developed into the "tassets" or little tabs, worn by men and women for the next fifty years or so. The basic pattern for these consists merely of the peplum cut into four or more pieces, lined and stiffened, and edged with braid or fringe. Reference to the costume books will indicate where modifications in size may be introduced.

Sleeves were plain in cut, but ornamented with braid or galloon in either vertical or horizontal stripes; the wrist ruffle was replaced by a lace-edged cuff which matched the standing "whisk" collar, and the stiff cartwheel ruff gave way to the falling ruff, which is similar in execution, but made of softer material. Lace-edged muslin, tightly gathered, can be used instead of the stiff pleated tarlatan.

The most marked change was in the trunk hose, which became longer and fuller. Sometimes they were padded, but this is unnecessary if a fairly substantial brocade is used. The pyjama-leg pattern serves to cut what is virtually an exaggerated pair of bloomers which may either be gathered with elastic just above the knee, or pleated into a narrow band to fasten just below the knee. Fig. 61 suggests how the basic pattern can be adapted; if gathered into a band, cut the breeches slightly less full, and leave a 4 in. slit in the side seam, to fasten with hooks and eyes. Garters of soft silk, edged with fringe, were worn with these breeches.

Felt hats, plumed and jewelled, continued to be worn, as did cloaks, though the latter were longer, reaching to the knees. Use the same method as already described for the flared cloak, with collar, in Chapter Four, and cut as in Fig. 62.

Hats remain pretty much the same, and cause no difficulty,

FIG. 60. CAVALIER

but from this period on there is the problem of boots, which were much in fashion, and cannot be faked. The only possible compromise, if your "men" are girls in, say, a school production, is to utilize the now fashionable knee-length boots with a lace "collar." For an adult male cast, however, there is no alternative to hiring.

Gloves, with embroidered or fringed gauntlets remained in vogue, so that it is worth while to add these as a permanent feature of the wardrobe.

Women's dress varied very little, and again, the same basic cutting will serve. The cart-wheel farthingale remained in fashion because James I's queen, Anne of Denmark, favoured it, but after her death in 1619 it gradually disappeared, though the

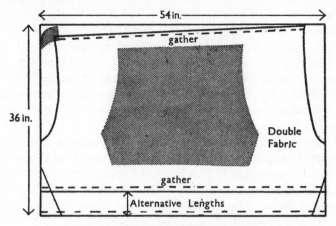

FIG. 61. JACOBEAN LOOSE BREECHES
Using either 36 or 45 in. fabric to equal three yards

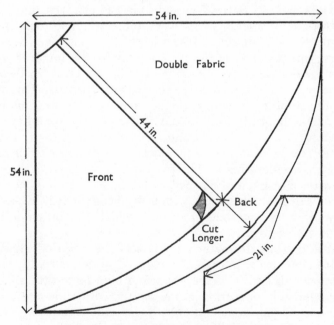

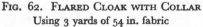

FIG. 62. FLARED CLOAK WITH COLLAR
Using 3 yards of 54 in. fabric

4

hip roll was still worn, as previously described in Chapter Four.

Gowns were still extremely décolleté—sometimes with a straight neckline, and later with a deep horseshoe line. If necessary a net fill-in can be added. Bodices retained the "dressing-table" frill, but this, too, disappeared with the farthingale. Sleeves followed much the same lines as the men's, with similar ornamentation and lace cuffs, and the "whisk" collar of lace was fashionable.

With the straight neckline, the ruff came right down to the front of the bodice, but with the later U-shaped neck, the standing collar reached only just beyond the shoulder seam. This is not an easy effect to achieve, and the wire or whalebone must be continued into the bodice lining, as previously described, to prevent the fan-shaped collar falling backwards.

Since skirts were now slightly shorter, shoes must be considered, and large ribbon rosettes, added to a strap shoe with a moderate heel, will achieve the right effect.

The reign of Charles I brought marked changes, though the alterations in men's styles were more gradual than in the women's. The doublet, with tassels of various sizes, was still worn, but the style of the sleeves went back a hundred years, and the double sleeve, described in Fig. 35, Chapter Two, reappears, with its top slightly enlarged and "paned." This again is quite simple to do, with appliqué bands of contrasting material.

Collars flopped, and so did ruffs; baggy breeches were severely pruned; they became very much narrower, though not as skin tight as later on, and are still within the scope of the average needlewoman. The pyjama pattern is pared down as shown in Fig. 63, and finished with a band fastening below the knee. The silk sash garters, with fringed ends are still in keeping, as well as the lace boot-hose tops, which can be made from nylon embroidery.

It is the last dramatic ten years of the reign of Charles I which show a considerable change. The doublet with tassels disappeared, and its place was taken by a loose-fitting jacket, usually of silk or satin in pastel shades, with cuffs and a deep falling collar of lace (Fig. 64). This, with variations of trimming, is the typical "Cavalier" costume, and though it does require more careful cutting and fitting, it is still well within the scope of the wardrobe mistress. Use pieces (A), (B), (C) and (D) of the basic pattern, pyjama jacket length, shaped slightly to the waist. Line the jacket and interline the front with iron-on interfacing. To save time, it is still permissible to make up lining and jacket as one piece, but the facing must be put on

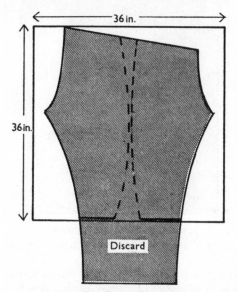

FIG. 63. PLAIN BREECHES
Using 2 yards of 36 in. or 1½ yards of 45 in. cloth, cut on dotted line

by the conventional method, and the back neck finished off with the curved facing-piece which should be slip-stitched back on to the lining.

This jacket was frequently worn open, with only the neck buttons fastened, and a separate shirt is necessary, with a lace collar and cuffs, which will show below the three-quarter length coat sleeve. As plain white shirts are useful stable items, it is worth making them to last. The lace collars and cuffs need only to be tacked on. Use either an ordinary shirt pattern, or the pyjama-coat, and use the pyjama collar, considerably enlarged, as a guide to cutting the lace collar.

Some portraits show a slashed coat sleeve, buttoned and braided, with about 9 buttons, the lower 6 being left unfastened, showing the white shirt. This is an extremely easy and effective

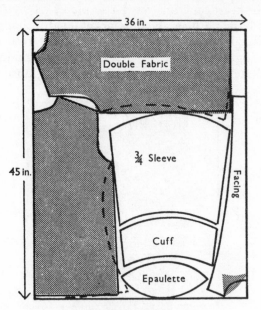

FIG. 64. CAVALIER JACKET
Using 2½ yards of 36 in. cloth, or 2 yards of 45 in.

"slash." Using piece (D) of the basic pattern, cut sleeve and lining; place lining on top of sleeve, right sides facing, and cut through both pieces from shoulder downwards, from a point midway between shoulder seam and the front "matching notch" on the basic pattern. Machine lining to sleeve along both sides of slash, press and turn inwards. Catch together for about 1½ in. top and bottom.

For the sleeve cuff, use the cuff pattern in Fig. 1, reduced to about 5 in. finished width. Cut two pieces, with an interlining. Tack or iron interfacing to the undercuff; join the short edges of upper- and undercuff, to make two circles. Join these together on the top edge, right sides together; press seams open and turn right-side out. Join sleeve to jacket, tack and fit; join side and underarm seams, and press. Join cuff to *inside* of sleeve, turn sleeve right-side out, pull the cuff through and turn it back, concealing the raw edges. Oversew the raw edges if they are inclined to fray. This apparently slip-shod method is, in fact, quite frequently used on manufactured

garments in the cheaper range, and avoids a bulky seam which
can result from the more orthodox way.

Epaulettes, trimmed with matching galloon, can be incor-
porated in the armhole seam, and should be cut from the

FIG. 65. "HENRIETTA MARIA" STYLE

pattern in Fig. 53, omitting the padding, but stiffened with
interlining.

The broad-brimmed black felt or velour hat, with a curling
plume pinned with a glittering jewel, completes the dashing
Cavalier costume.

From France came Henrietta Maria, bringing with her
some welcome changes. Farthingales were out, the long
waist and stomacher were soon discarded—probably with
relief, since they must have been extremely uncomfortable—
and the waist line resumed its natural place. However, these

gowns were worn over numerous petticoats, and to achieve this effect without bulk, a modified version of the hip roll is still required. Make this as described in Chapter Ten, but use considerably less padding.

Fabrics were generally unpatterned, and soft in texture, and as with the men's costumes, the predominant feature was fine lace. This is a charming and simple period to costume, and the basic pattern needs very little modification.

Use the standard skirt pattern Fig. 29, Chapter Two, with slightly less fullness. It can be made separately if intended for wear with a bodice with lappets; otherwise, make up as instructed in Chapter Two. The practice of wearing the skirt open down the front to show the petticoat was now so infrequent that it can be discarded as an unnecessary complication, though some portraits do depict the skirt caught up at each side to show a contrasting petticoat. If this variation is used, the petticoat need be no more than a deep flounce attached to a stock petticoat, and the tassets should be omitted. Use pieces (A) and (B) of basic pattern. The only modification required is the neckline, which is wide and almost off the shoulders. It may be either square or curved, and as previously mentioned, the back of the bodice must be cut high enough to prevent it slipping off the shoulders, as in Fig. 66. Finish the neckline either with small vandykes of lace, or a falling collar of lace.

Sleeves were now considerably simpler, with very little ornamentation beyond a lace frill. In cut they were similar to the puffed sleeves worn in the 1930's, reaching to the elbow or a little below. Use the basic sleeve (G), adapted as in Fig. 66, cut a similar interlining, and mount on to a plain lining, as shown for the upper part of Fig. 35. The frill may be a double layer of lace, nylon frilling or curtain net, and, as the lower edge of the sleeve is itself fairly full to begin with, it is unnecessary to use more than this width. Tack frill to the right side of the sleeve, raw edges together, and draw up to fit the lower edge of the sleeve lining. Machine together, sandwiching the frill between lining and sleeve.

The portraits of the time show in considerable detail what ornamentation is suitable. Ribbon sashes, with matching bows down the front of the bodice, are in keeping, and need no description.

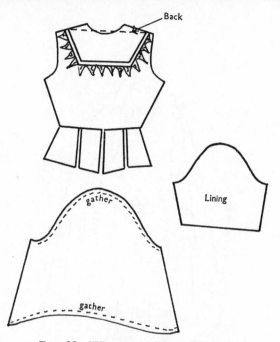

FIG. 66. "HENRIETTA MARIA" BODICE

The ladies continued to borrow their hat styles from the men and, for riding, wore the wide-brimmed, befeathered Cavalier hat. Otherwise, head-covering was not fashionable, and did not extend beyond a loosely draped gauze veil, or, in winter, a hood of velvet, satin or silk, possibly matching the cloak.

During the Commonwealth dress, both men's and women's, was pruned of fripperies, though not as drastically as is generally supposed. Reference to authoritative costume books and to contemporary paintings show that England did not become uniformly Puritan with one stroke of the axe in 1649. The more austere of the Parliamentarians cropped their hair, wore hard, high-crowned felt hats, and sober, plain-cut breeches and jackets with a severe white linen falling collar, and cuffs. Wives obediently, if sometimes reluctantly, followed their husbands' example.

For stage purposes there emerges the generally accepted "Quaker Girl" set of costumes, so severe as to present no

FIG. 67. PURITAN MAN

difficulty in cutting, but requiring more meticulous tailoring, with no ornamentation or gathering to cover any deficiencies in marrying sleeve to jacket, etc.

The jacket should be slightly longer than the Cavalier jacket, and made to button down the front; the side seam is left open for about 12 in. and finished off with buttons and sham button holes.

Breeches can be either tight-fitting below the knee, or a little wider, and not gathered into a band. Both can be cut as already described, and either left plain, or finished with little looped tabs.

Cloaks can be plain, and less voluminous, and a cloak as

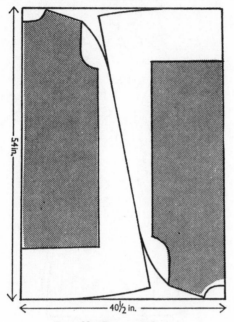

FIG. 68. PURITAN CLOAK
Using 2¼ yards of 54 in. cloth

shown in Fig. 68 can be cut from 2¼ yards of 54 in. material, used widthways.

The Puritan's wife stripped her gown of every iota of ornament. She wore drab grey, of severe cut, with long sleeves and plain white collar and cuffs, and probably a plain white apron and cap. If she wore a hat, it was the same as her husband's, and worn over her cap.

However, these extreme styles are more or less caricatures of what was actually worn. The Royalists bided their time, and went on wearing their Godless attire—a little shabby, maybe, after years of civil war and the resultant sequestration of estates.

All that is necessary in actual production is a careful differentiation between the two sides by colour and trimming, or lack of it. The Royalists wore shorter jackets, open down the front, sometimes with the slashed sleeve; the ends of tubular breeches

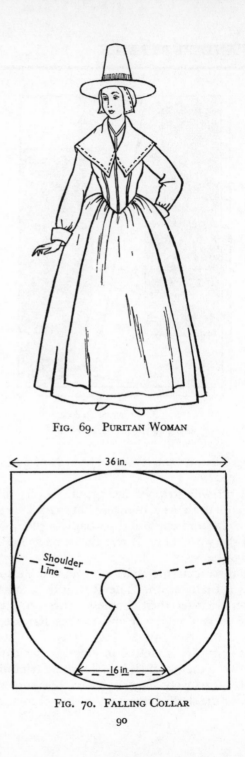

FIG. 69. PURITAN WOMAN

36 in.

Shoulder
Line

16 in.

FIG. 70. FALLING COLLAR

90

were trimmed with ribbon loops, and a bunch of similar loops also adorned the top of the breeches, where the jacket fell open. Cloaks were slightly shorter than those worn by the other side, and had a brightly contrasting lining and a larger collar.

There was very little actual change in women's styles— merely the toning down by the more sober-minded. Necklines remained low, but were mostly concealed by a double lace-edged collar, rather like a small cape. The Royalist lady wore more lace, perhaps three tiers and left her collar open in an inverted V-front. Cut this collar as in Fig. 70, reducing the depth of the second and third tiers.

The Royalist lady also wore a white apron, but it was a mere gesture of lace-trimmed muslin.

So, until 1660, Fashion sat it out, primly, but waiting.

CHAPTER SIX

RESTORATION TO QUEEN ANNE

THE Restoration of the monarchy and the return of the Stuarts brought a very strong reaction towards luxury, and men's attire became most effeminate and fantastic.

The jacket shrank to a bolero, leaving visible a billowing white shirt above petticoat-breeches, which had no division

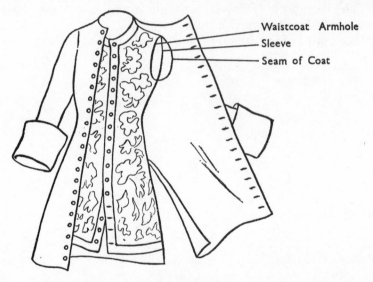

Waistcoat Armhole
Sleeve
Seam of Coat

FIG. 71. WAISTED COAT WITH SIDE SLASH AND BROCADED LONG WAISTCOAT

and were worn over close-fitting underpants. Loops of ribbon sprouted everywhere, singly, and in bunches, edging the breeches, top and bottom, and arranged in overlapping tiers up the front. Sleeves, slashed, cuffed, and trimmed with bows, were three-quarter length, displaying more shirt sleeve, with a deep wrist-ruffle of lace. The whole absurd confection was finished off with lace ruffles below the knee.

The abbreviated jacket was superseded by the coat, introduced by Charles II. By 1670, the coat and vest were generally worn, and in one form or another, have remained standard wear for men ever since.

At first the coat hung loosely from the shoulders, to about knee-length. It is basically, in cut, the tunic of Fig. 4, centuries removed by the mere change in fabric and trimming. Velvet, face-cloth or satin were used, richly lined, the lining turned back in a tuxedo front, with deep slits at the sides and back, ornately trimmed with braid frogging, and, just within reach of the finger-tips, a braid-trimmed pocket.

Sleeves were elbow length (the basic pattern, shortened, will serve) with turned-back cuffs, for which the cuff pattern in Fig. 1 should be used.

The usual frilled shirt was worn, with a large portion of sleeve showing, and the neck of the coat was collarless, with a lace-trimmed cravat.

Beneath the coat, a waistcoat or vest is necessary. This need only be a sham, attached to the coat at the shoulder, front arm-hole and side seams (it must be attached to the *back* of the jacket below the split). The vest, of contrasting brocade, fastens right down the front and is only a couple of inches shorter than the coat.

Breeches were plain, similar in cut to those described in the previous chapter, finished with a band below the knee, and sash garters. Cloaks were still in vogue, reaching a little below the hem of the coat.

There was still a spattering of bows—on the shoulder, at the knee, on the shoes and on the hat, which was plain and low-crowned. It is, of course, necessary to complete the effect with the full, curled wig.

From now on, the men's costumes need very careful fitting on the shoulders and across the back. It is also preferable to make the lining separately. Cut lining and coat exactly the same, but omit hem allowance from lining. Assemble each in the follow-ing order. Join shoulder seams and press; insert sleeves and press; join in one operation the underarm seam and the side seam as far as the slit—about half-way between armhole and hem. Press side seams of lining and of coat (unless it is velvet, in which case, flatten seams with thumb-nail). At the same time, press back the seam allowances of the slits, since this makes it much easier to slip-stitch the lining into place. But

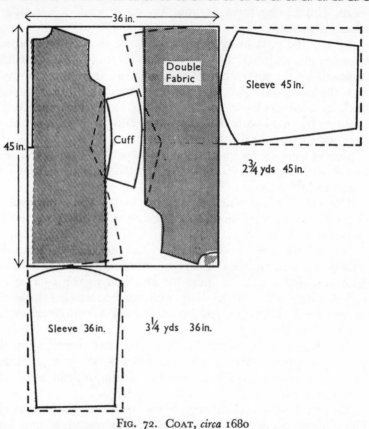

FIG. 72. COAT, *circa* 1680
Showing alternatives for cutting 36 in. and 45 in. fabric

before dealing with the slits, pin or tack the lining to the coat, right sides together, and machine up one front, round the neck and down the other front. Clip curved neck portions and turn coat right side out. Press, and machine all round about $\frac{1}{2}$ in. from edge. Turn wrong-side out, and tack the side seams of lining to the side seams of coat—this is a rather awkward job, as both fronts will be sandwiched between the back portions of coat and lining, but it is worth the extra trouble as it stops the lining from slithering about, and improves the roll of the tuxedo.

Turn up a 3 in. hem and slip-stitch; also slip-stitch lining into place along hem line and up the slits, taking care that the lower edge does not drag in wear. Turn back tuxedo front and trim with braid, bobble fringe and mock buttonholes. Use braid for sham pocket openings.

Instructions for sleeves and cuffs are common to this and the ensuing styles, so are given later in this chapter.

By about 1680 a slightly waisted effect was becoming fashionable; over the next ten years or so coats became

FIG. 73. FLARED COAT SHOWING INSET GODET

progressively more fitted at the waist, and consequently increasingly flared, still with slits, for ease of walking. The basic method of cutting and making remains the same, the wider skirted effect being achieved by cutting in to the waist, as indicated by the broken line in Fig. 72.

Finally, round about 1689, the coat settled into a style which lasted, with minor variations, for the next 100 years or so.

Cutting becomes slightly more complicated; the basic pattern no longer suffices, and it is necessary to use a tailored jacket pattern with a panelled back and a two-piece sleeve. The typical feature of this style is the godet set in the side-back seams. The sweep of the flare may be as much as a half-circle.

Cut the body of the jacket from a purchased pattern, extending to required length—the bend of the knee plus a 3 in. hem allowance. Shape side-seam in sharply to the waist, and swing out to bottom hem. For inset godet cut two quarter- or half-circles, according to available material, using a radius equal to the measurement from hip-bone to hem, allowing only a normal turning, not a 3 in. hem, which is extremely awkward to turn up on a circular line. The front of the coat is plain, without the tuxedo effect, and there is no collar, so cut to the pattern, with a facing, but omitting collar (Fig. 74). Assemble in the following order—

Make the godets first. Place godet lining, right side up, flat on table, and mark four radial lines at 18°, 36°, 54° and 72° (see diagram), using either tailor's chalk, pencil or ball-point pen, as the marks will not show in wear.

Match godet to lining, right sides together, and join on curved edge. Trim seam to ¼ in., turn right side out and press, smoothing lining in an upward direction towards the point. Place flat on table, tack lining to godet along both straight edges, and tack through lining and main fabric along the previously marked lines. Taking each line in turn, fold, with lining *outside*, press, and machine ⅜ in. from edge, from hem to within 1 in. of point. Press into sunray pleats.

Join centre back seam, leaving a slit as before. On side-back sections of back, mark the hem-allowance on side-back seam, and join godet to main piece from this point; machine to within ⅝ in. of point of godet. Now join back section to side back. Place the side-back section (with the godet already attached) uppermost, pin downwards from armhole, and match the end of the godet to a previously measured point on the back section equal to "radius + hem." Pin this point at right-angles to raw edge, and carefully drop machine-needle to the last stitch of the previous seam. Machine from this point upwards; pull threads through and tie off, and turn garment over. With centre-back section uppermost, machine the other edge of the godet to the main garment, again taking care that the needle starts exactly on the last stitch of the previous row of machining. (Push the other turnings to the left, out of the way.)

Join shoulder and side seams; make up sleeves also—since with a two-piece sleeve the underarm and side seams do not coincide, the sleeves must be inserted in the orthodox way. Attach the cuff *before* inserting sleeves into coat. Join sleeve seams and seams of lining; turn lining with seams inwards, but leave the coat sleeve inside out and slide into lining,

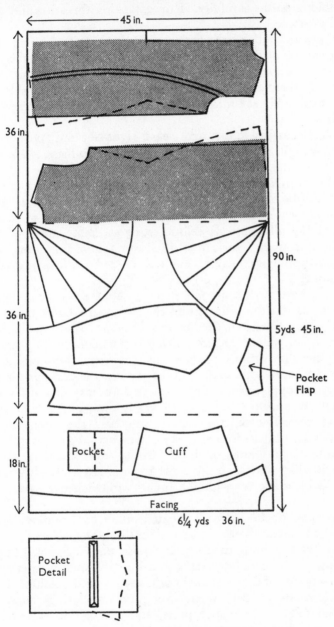

FIG. 74. BASIC FLARED COAT

matching seams carefully. Run a tacking thread round wrist and armhole.

Make up cuff by method previously described. The inner cuff can be of the same material as the coat lining, making it less cumbersome. With cuff and sleeve *both* inside out, drop sleeve into cuff and machine firmly. Pull sleeve right side out, and turn cuff back into position, catching into place on sleeve seams.

With coat inside out and sleeve right-side out, push sleeve up through armhole, ease in shoulder fullness, tack and machine.

Make up lining, joining shoulder, centre-back, and side-back seams. Machine inner edge of facing to front of lining. Press seam allowance on lining. Attach facing and lining to coat by machining all round as before; turn up hem, and slip-stitch lining into place; turn in and fell armhole of lining over raw edges, clipping on curves. Fell lower side back over raw edges of godets.

This, basically, is the jacket until about 1790. The length varied, as did the fullness and the size of the cuffs, but all of these points can be checked by reference to the costume books—Doreen Yarwood's *English Costume* is particularly informative, and the illustrations provide all necessary guidance as to trimming and accessories. Truman's *Historic Costuming* is also useful in supplying a comprehensive summary of the fashions of this period, up to 1820, particularly the waistcoats or vests. These varied considerably in length, and the later, shorter styles had cutaway fronts. They can be actual garments, made separately, or shams, made as "fronts" and attached at side and shoulder seams. If the latter method is adopted, the sham should be made up with the lining, sandwiched between the seams.

Pockets can be shams, indicated either by braiding, or by attached pocket-flaps. Where essential, the pocket must be made before joining the front at side-seam. Cut pocket flap as in Fig. 74—fabric, interfacing and lining. Anchor interfacing to wrong side of flap with tacks or Copydex, and machine lining (fabric sandwiched between lining and interfacing) all round shaped edges. Turn and press, and run a line of machine stitching all round.

Cut pocket lining as shown in diagram, and mark centre line as indicated. Mark position of pocket on coat front with either a chalk line or a tacking thread. Tack pocket-flap to coat, with raw edge downwards and just meeting tacking line. Place pocket lining on top, right sides facing, with the marked centre line corresponding to the marking thread on coat, and tack. Machine in a rectangle (as when making a buttonhole) taking in $\frac{1}{4}$ in. along raw edge of pocket flap, turn, and machine $\frac{5}{8}$ in. at right angles, turn and machine parallel to first line, turn and complete rectangle. Slash as indicated in diagram, and pull lining through to inside. Match raw edges and machine together to form pocket. Press pocket flaps downwards and catch to short edges of rectangle.

Some sketches show the pocket opening above the flap. The method of making is the same, but the operation must be reversed and the flap placed on the coat right side up. Complete as before, roll flap upwards to cover slit, stitch, and turn back.

The fashionable hat was the tricorne, easy to contrive from a velour or felt hat. Trimmings were various—ostrich feather fringe, petersham ribbon, gold braid, again the books will give you the answer.

Cloaks, long enough to cover the coat, were still worn in winter, and the stock pattern and method can be used. Boots are no longer necessary, but shoes are now rather a problem, as they ought really to have squarish toes and heels considerably higher than present-day wear. If the real thing is absolutely essential, there is really no alternative to hiring, but a good imitation, though without the high heel, can be made by attaching a leather or plastic flap and buckle to a plain "monk" shoe.

The early Restoration styles for women show very little initial change, beyond the disappearance of the broad lace collar. The neckline remained wide and décolleté, finished with a narrow ruffle; the bodice was still close-fitting, and once more tapered to a point in front. Skirts were voluminous, and sleeves puffed. Occasionally a contrasting white silk or cambric sleeve, also puffed, showed below the main sleeve. In actual cutting there is therefore nothing new. The pointed bodice is similar to the Tudor line, as is the full skirt, and the puffed

FIG. 75. LACE FONTANGE WORN WITH MARY II GOWN

sleeves are also an echo of an earlier fashion. Modified hip pads are still necessary to give the effect of numerous petticoats, which still showed beneath the raised skirt, so the false valance can be used.

By about 1670 fashion settled into a style which, with minor variations, lasted into the Hanoverian period.

The bodice remained pointed, the neckline hardly changed at all, neither did the sleeves, but the petticoat was very much in evidence, important enough to be a whole garment in its own right. It may be finished with a small frill, and is best made in a soft, pastel material contrasting with the gown, the skirt of which is slit up the front, looped back with large bows, and long enough to form a train.

The basic methods already described still suffice, and reference to earlier chapters will show how to adapt and cut. The underskirt should consist of either 3 yards of 45 in. material used widthways, or three widths of 36 in. material of requisite

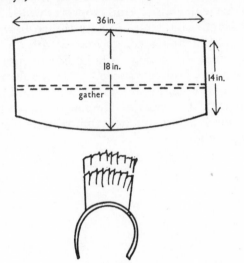

FIG. 76. FONTANGE

length. For the skirt of the main gown, use the "standard" skirt in Fig. 29. Up till the reign of Anne, a hip roll was still worn.

Sleeves now became quite plain, elbow length, with a fairly deep ruffle; sometimes small cuffs were added, with bows to match those catching back the skirt.

The tiny, lace-edged apron was typical of the reigns of William and Mary and of Anne—so much so that it is almost an integral part of the dress, being tucked under the point of the bodice. Bows of ribbon ornamented the front of the bodice, the shoulders, sleeves, and the skirt, and after over 100 years, the cap reappeared—a very light and frothy confection of lace, known as a fontange. This can be a double frill of lace pleated on to an Alice band. Allow about 1½ yards of stiff lace, nylon embroidery, or net; cut into two equal pieces, and trim one piece 2 in. narrower. Join long edges, roll-hem short edges, and box-pleat along join, reducing to about 7 in. Sew firmly to Alice band, pull upright, and catch frills together in between the pleats. If made of net, stiff nylon embroidery, or starched lace, it should not be necessary to wire the fontange. To complete the cap, make either a little muslin "pill-box" to cover the back of the head, or a circle of net, muslin or lace, and draw up to size with elastic. Add lappets of wide lace insertion, to shoulder length, and trim cap with ribbon bows (Fig. 76).

The stomacher reappeared, decorated with an "échelle" or ladder of graduated flat bows, the bodice being laced across, and also the hoop, a direct descendant of the farthingale, and quite obviously the mother of the crinoline and bustle. These are all dealt with in a separate chapter, to avoid repetition of instructions for making up, but approximate dates for each variation will be given.

CHAPTER SEVEN

HANOVERIAN

THE new dynasty brought no startling changes in men's dress until part way through the reign of George III.

Then the brittle, witty world splintered. Revolution and the ensuing war cut us off from the French influence so long predominant, and the rest of the Hanoverian period laid the foundation of English tailoring.

Adult costumes require an increasing degree of tailoring ability, but are well within the capacity of any dressmaker who can tackle a tailored suit or coat. The correct effect is achieved by judicious choice of material, and a firm interlining will give the illusion of solidity.

By about 1780, the enormous cuffs and flares had disappeared, and collars appeared for the first time as part of the jacket itself, which crystallized into the frock-coat similar to present-day ceremonial Court dress, and later into the cut-away tail coat with broad lapels and collar still preserved in formal evening wear. Sleeves were plain, without cuffs, and waistcoats gradually shrivelled to waist length.

Breeches were knee-length, until about 1790, when full-length trousers edged their way in. In the 1820's these parvenus achieved permanent status following "Prinny's" lead.

Because of the similarity to present-day wear, cutting is not such a problem, and modern patterns of the correct size will need very little adaptation to achieve the illusion of an earlier era.

The early tail-coat had no *revers*; the collar, usually of velvet, ran straight into the front edge, and Fig. 78 shows how to adapt the basic pattern. The necessity for a close fit must be kept in mind, and a smaller size used. Because of the "tails," a centre back seam is essential, and a coat pattern with a back vent will give clear and detailed directions for making.

It is not a practical proposition to embark on meticulous and authentic tailoring methods, but careful observation, added to

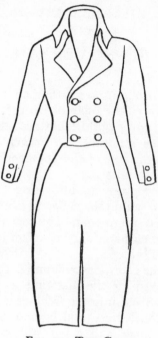

FIG. 77. TAIL COAT

ingenuity in improvisation, will produce passable imitations which will not disgrace a production.

With such a mass of evidence as is now available in portraits, books, and museums of costume, it is impossible to cover the field in detail, since every decade brings minor variations.

Break up the basic pattern into eight component parts for the body of the coat—upper front, upper side back, back panel, with the lower front and lower side back in one piece. It will sometimes be necessary to cut the centre back panel in four pieces (upper and lower sections), but this will be obvious from a study of the relevant fashion plate. The two-section sleeve is cut from the conventional pattern, widened or narrowed as required.

Assemble in the following order: join centre-back seam *g–h*; turn under and slip-stitch left side of vent; face right hand side of vent. Join *d–e* to *d'–e'* and, if following diagram (i), clip corner at *e'* and join *e–b* to *e'–b'*; if following diagram (ii),

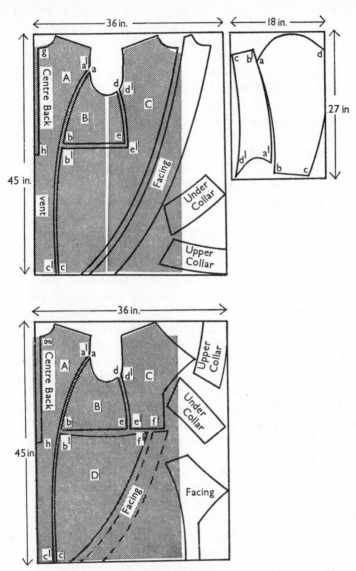

FIG. 78. TAIL COAT
This shows the basic cut. See reference books for variations.
Upper diagram (i); lower diagram (ii)

join *f–b* to *f'–b'*. Join *a–c* to *a'–c'* and make a small pleat (facing towards centre back) at point *b*; join shoulder seams; join under-collar to main garment and upper collar to facing—most patterns include a shaped "back-neck" facing which meets the facing at the shoulder seam, so join these pieces before attaching collar. The front facing should continue in one piece right down piece *D* to point (*c*), but piece *A* is finished with a hem as deep as the width of the facing.

Unless the actual role calls for taking the coat off on stage, much work on the lining can be by-passed. Cut the lining exactly the same as the coat, and make up as one piece of fabric, even to the point of joining the facing all round the outer edge and then turning it inwards and slip-stitching it to the lining, which will stay in place because it is already anchored at the seams. Line the sleeves before inserting.

The variations in cut can be picked up from the experts, and quite the most helpful book I have found is Norah Waugh's *The Cut of Men's Clothes—1600–1900*. This deals in great detail with a comprehensive and representative range of men's costumes, even showing some of the very early pattern layouts, as well as illustrations of cravats and collars.

These instructions apply by-and-large to all the men's wear of the period. The most notable later alterations were the widening of lapels, larger collars, and cut-away fronts, and the substitution of trousers for breeches. Overcoats instead of cloaks now become the accepted outer wear, and quite frequently they had three-tier cape-collars reaching almost to the elbow. The same basic methods apply, and the cape is a curtailed version of the round Elizabethan cape.

The characteristic tricorne hat was worn until about the 1780's, and can be made from an old trilby or a felt hood, as can the later fashion of the bicorne, which was at different times worn with the points at the side, particularly in the French Revolution period, or with the points fore and aft, a fashion still cherished by our admirals. The more exaggerated style associated with the Revolution is made by attaching to a soft felt crown a crescent-shaped brim cut from matching felt and stuck with Copydex on to buckram for extra body. Fig. 80 shows how to cut this.

Also in fashion, and by about 1789 replacing the tricorne,

FIG. 79. BICORNE HAT

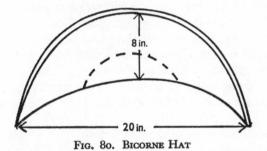

8 in.

20 in.

FIG. 80. BICORNE HAT

was a felt hat with a high crown and rolled brim. This, too, can be evolved from the trilby by steaming thoroughly and blocking on an inverted flower-pot. (Use steam from the spout of a kettle, do *not* soak it in hot water.) Get a constant jet of steam, but take very great care not to burn your fingers— steam burns are worse than ordinary burns. The easiest way is to hold the hat by the brim and direct the jet into the crown; then fit it over the flower-pot and gently stretch downwards. Trim with petersham ribbon and a buckle.

Women's costumes, while remaining the same in essentials,

became progressively more elaborate. From the eighteenth century onwards, a sufficient number of gowns has survived to present an accurate picture of high fashion, one of the most comprehensive collections being at the Victoria and Albert Museum in London and its branch at Bethnal Green.

The predominant features were the hoop (dealt with in detail in a separate chapter) and the saque, which was exactly what it sounds like—a sack. It was at first a loose, shapeless overgown, with or without sleeves according to taste, gathered into the neck, back and front; it soon became fashionable to wear it open to the waist, displaying the stomacher. Then the fashionable woman nipped the sack at the waist, and arranged the back fullness into "Watteau" pleats.

The original sack is the full Plantagenet gown of Fig. 16, preferably without sleeves, for ease of changing. Any fairly thin, soft fabric is suitable, and a plain taffeta with a design painted round the bottom is not out of character, since painted fabric was very much the vogue in this era. This "over-all" sack can also be cut with a narrower front, having a deep "V" to the waist. To prevent slipping in wear, hold it in place with concealed press-studs at waist and shoulders.

Eventually the sack became the gown proper, by which time the hoop had become flattened back and front, but widened to such an extent that the width of the gown sometimes exceeded the length from waist to ground. Such extravagance is best avoided, and a three-yard hoop is about the maximum practicable.

The bodice front is the same as before, with a very low neckline and a separate V-shaped stomacher. The sack-back is sewn to the lining, to form the pleats. Fig. 82 shows the component parts of the sack, which are assembled into a coat-like gown fastening centre front at the waist. The side-fronts of the bodice then hook on to the stomacher, the point of which is slightly below the waist, projecting free over the top of the underskirt; alternatively, the gown may be tied across the stomacher with ribbons.

(Instructions for making the stomacher are given in the chapter on Elizabethan costume.)

The shaded sections in Fig. 82 indicate the basic pattern. Cut the bodice back and front of the gown as shown by black

FIG. 81. SACQUE (*Sack*) GOWN

lines *a–b* and *f–h*. (Compare with piece *6*—the centre portion of the bodice back is dispensed with, thus eliminating one thickness.) Cut front lining the same as bodice front, but cut back bodice lining entire, as piece *6* on diagram. Mark line *a–b* with tacking thread or ball-point pen.

Cut skirt as piece *3*, and trim on line *g–i*, leaving centre front (*f–i*) open to show contrasting underskirt. *NOTE:* with 36 in. material, cut three lengths of 1½ yards each; divide one piece in half lengthways (parallel with selvedges) and join one piece to each of the other two pieces, making two squares each 1½ × 1½ yards. Trim away on line *g–i* and hem fronts.

Join *b–c* to *b'–c'*. Join piece *4*, *a'–g'* to bodice and skirt on line *a–g*. Tack bodice of gown to bodice lining round armhole and down side seam, then tack and machine bodice gown to

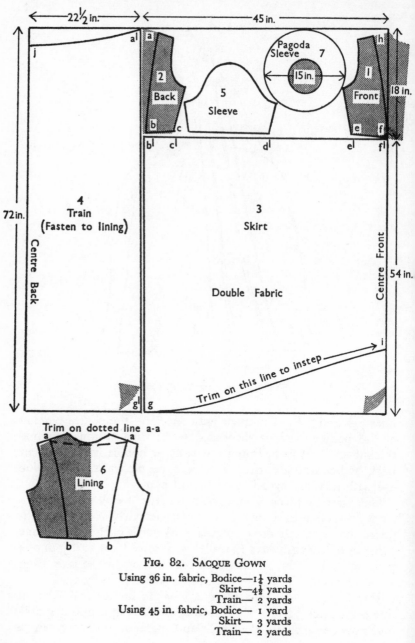

FIG. 82. SACQUE GOWN

Using 36 in. fabric, Bodice—1¼ yards
Skirt—4⅓ yards
Train— 2 yards
Using 45 in. fabric, Bodice— 1 yard
Skirt— 3 yards
Train— 2 yards

bodice lining on line *a–b*. This attaches the train from neck to
waist, leaving the lower part of the train floating. Pleat the
surplus at line *a–j* to fit neck line along the lining. About
three large box pleats will give the typical "Watteau" line as
in Fig. 81. The neckline can be finished either with a "curtain
frill" effect, or ruching to match bodice.

Join the bodice to the skirt, *e–f* to *e'–f'*; join the shoulder
seams and insert sleeve; join underarm and side seams. This
brings point *e* to point *c*; machine from this point along the top
of the skirt to point *d*. This seam sits along the centre of the
pannier, and the end point is pushed inwards under the seam;
form small, radiating pleats, two back and two front, to fit over
the rounded ends of the hoop.

Study of actual costumes confirms that for general wear a
much smaller hoop was used, with considerably less material
in the skirt. Instead of the top-seam method, the side fullness
of the sack gown was pleated in under the side seam of the
bodice, and provided the material used is thin, this is quite
effective. Form a bunch of pleats *before* attaching the bodice,
tack firmly, then turn under the seam allowance on the bodice,
and welt-stitch over the skirt.

Finally, the sack back may be a separate train, pleated from
the shoulder, caught in at the waist, with the remaining length
free. Use the full width of material, preferably 45–48 in., and
allow a length equal to the measurement from shoulder to
ground, plus as long a train as is manageable—up to about
36 in.

With a flimsy material a lining may be necessary, but a
brocade will suffice with a deep hem, and either should be
weighted.

Sleeves remained elbow length, plain and close-fitting,
trimmed with either a broad cuff, or a "pagoda" flounce (7),
made from a circle about 16 in. in diameter, with a hole in the
middle, slightly off centre. Attach to sleeve in the same way as
the falling sleeve in the Norman chapter, and trim with bow;
finish with inner lace frill or pleated silk flounce.

Trimmings were ornate, ruching being particularly used. If
the costume is to receive much wear, use thin taffeta ribbon,
allowing not less than double the required final length. Most
sewing machines have a gathering foot and some will take an

adjustable ruching attachment. Another effective trim can be made from net, which needs no hemming. Cut the net into strips of, say, 3 in.–5 in. and use double or more—in two colours, if desired. To trim the fronts and bottom hem of an overskirt, it is much easier to do it flat, before joining to the bodice. Start at the waist, and drop the presser-foot in the centre on the double net. Make a ¼ in. fold across the strip, run a couple of stitches through it and continue ¼ in. pinch pleats about 1 in. apart, all down the front, along bottom hem, and up the other front. There is no need to join the net strips together first—push each new piece ¼ in. under the previous one. Do not run the machine too fast and keep the pleats at regular intervals. Before making up, trim the front of the bodice and the sleeves in the same way. Leave the pleated net flat until the garment is finished, then gently pull the layers apart. Alternatively, pleat the net or ribbon along one edge, then go back and pleat the other edge in the reverse direction.

Taffeta, cut into narrow strips with pinking shears, can also be used, and it is these variations in trimming which transform the basic gown into the elaborate confection of a Pompadour or a Du Barry.

Contemporary with these elaborate styles was the mock simplicity of Marie Antoinette's "milk-maid" whim, with the over-skirt looped up in festoons. Mark four points, level with bodice darts, and run vertical double gathering threads half-way up the skirt. Draw up tightly and trim with contrasting bow.

These skirts were considerably shorter, about ankle-length, and high-heeled shoes are not out of place.

About the 1780's a simpler trend developed. Hoops retired in favour of a bustle, for which half of the kidney-shaped Tudor hip-pad will suffice. The sack-back was discarded, and the fullness of the skirt, instead of being concentrated at the sides, was evenly distributed in tiny ¼ in. pinch-pleats; the bodice came to a sharp point at the centre back, about 6–7 in. below the waist-line. The skirt is a straight piece, with the short edges angled slightly outwards. This allows for the point of the bodice and retains selvedges top and bottom, thus avoiding fraying. Round off the point at centre back hem. The skirt will fall into a small train at the back (Fig. 83).

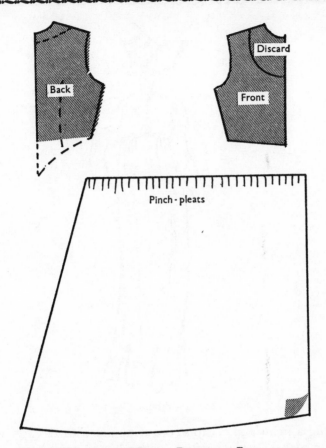

FIG. 83. GOWN WITH BUSTLE BACK WITH PINCH-PLEATS
Yardage as for sacque without train

The bodice was still close-fitting, with frilled sleeves, and a
plunge neckline trimmed with a fichu, which requires no
"making" at all. Use 1 yard of curtain net with a frilled edge,
folded in half, with the upper frill just slightly overlapping the
lower one. Gather raw edges and attach centre front, concealing join with a bow.

This gown can be worn without a bustle, and the bodice may
be slightly high-wasited, with a broad contrasting sash. It is a
style which lends itself very well to improvisation, since an old
evening dress cut on these lines is very easily converted by

FIG. 84. EMPIRE GOWN

adding a fichu and a cap sleeve trimmed with lace. A wide-brimmed hat in black velvet, with plumes, completed a very charming costume, reminiscent of a Gainsborough portrait.

The 1790's brought in what was perhaps the most drastic change of fashion in history, the French Empire style.

Cut the bodice from the basic pattern, abbreviated as in Fig. 85. The waistline must be just under the bust, and fit tightly; the fullness is disposed of either by darts or pleats immediately under the bust or, if the material is fine enough, by close gathers radiating from the centre front. The skirt, which is cut from a straight piece, is attached to the bodice so that it hangs perfectly straight in front, the entire surplus fullness being concentrated in close gathers at the centre back; a ball gown may have a train of any manageable length.

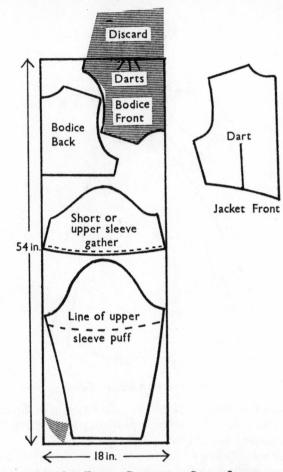

FIG. 85. EMPIRE GOWN WITH SHORT JACKET

For jacket use modified puffed sleeve as Fig. 35, and basic pattern for
back. Add mandarin collar, 2 in. deep. The jacket takes 2 yards of velvet.
For gown use 1½ yards of 36 in. or 45 in. fabric; plus 3¾ yards of 36 in. or
3 yards of 45 in. for skirt.

For evening wear, the neck-line can be wide and fairly
décolleté; for day wear, close to the neck, finished with a
small frill or plain collar; sleeves are very short and puffed,
and the day dress adds a long, close-fitting sleeve which is a
modification of the Plantagenet sleeve of Fig. 35, made up in
the same way.

Fig. 86. Queen Adelaide Gown

Use fine, soft nylon, Terylene lawn, fine rayon, or, for evening wear, curtain net. The latter is particularly effective if made up on a coloured foundation.

Outdoor wear followed the same lines, and rather attractive little jackets ending at the waist, as well as full-length coats, sometimes with cape collars, were very fashionable. For these, the basic bodice pattern is adequate. A pelisse or cape, cut as the Elizabethan cape, elbow length, is also in keeping.

By the 1820's the waist-line had dropped, bodices were close fitting, and skirts began to "bell" again, although the hoop had not yet returned, the skirt being held out by starched petticoats. It is better to adhere to the real thing and wear a stiffened petticoat, even if the stiffening is only newspaper, since a hoop betrays itself by a "swing" which immediately stamps it as an anachronism. The skirt should be shaped, not gathered, and

the basic flared skirt can be adapted. In the final decade of
this period skirts became progressively fuller, and the best way
to achieve this is a gathered flare, using four pieces cut from
piece (*E*) of the basic pattern.

Evening dresses still had low necks and puffed sleeves,

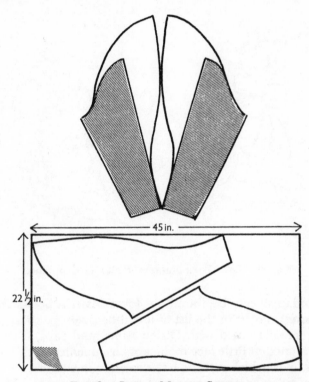

FIG. 87. LEG-OF-MUTTON SLEEVE
Using 1½ yards of 36 in. or 1 yard of 45 in. fabric

considerably enlarged; day dresses had a greatly exaggerated
version of the leg-of-mutton sleeve, cut from the basic pattern
modified as in Fig. 87. As this is a one-piece sleeve, it is not
possible to sustain the puff by mounting it on a lining as in
Fig. 35. It must be interlined with tarlatan, thin foam rubber
or Vilene. For the fine materials such as lawn, the iron-on
Vilene, though a little more expensive, is preferable. Iron-on
Staflex works very well with less flimsy materials, and another

type of "sleeve-extender" can be made from a pleated fan of double tarlatan sewn into the armhole.

Skirts were never much above the ankle.

Side by side with these fluctuations of style, headwear indulged in comparable vagaries, as did hair styles, on which

FIG. 88. *Left:* POKE BONNET; *Right:* CALASH HOOD

full guidance can be found in Joyce Asser's book, *Historic Hairdressing*, noted in the list of useful books on p. 160.

The fontange died with Queen Anne, and caps, if worn at all, were modest little lace mob-caps, ornamented with bows or flowers, over which a straw hat was worn in summer.

Hair styles became more and more extravagant. Hats, if any, were mere straw tokens, not much bigger than present-day carnival novelties, clinging precariously to a puffed and powdered precipice of hair, and nothing was too fantastic to serve as decoration. It was to protect these monumental coiffures that the calash hood was evolved. (The name does in fact also denote a carriage with a folding hood, alternatively, a calèche.)

The authentic calash was anything up to 22 in. high and 18 in. wide, supported on six whalebone arches, but such exaggeration will not often be required, unless for comic effect in pantomime. Whatever the size, the making is the same.

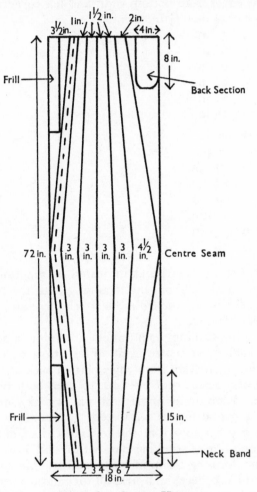

FIG. 89. CALASH HOOD

Divide four yards of ¼ in. feather-boning into five pieces: 2 × 27 in., 2 × 29 in., 1 × 31 in. Cut 1 yard of taffeta in half and join at selvedges with a ⅛ in. seam, making a 2-yard strip half a yard wide. Press seams with both edges the same way, to facilitate threading. Make a similar strip in white taffeta for the lining. Mark lines on lining as in Fig. 89 as follows:

On short edges from bottom right and left corners:

Mark 1   3½ in.   (½ in. turning)
    2   5 in.
    3   6½ in.
    4   8 in.
    5   9½ in.
    6   11 in.
    7   13 in.

On centre seam:

Mark 1   edge
    2   1½ in.
    3   4½ in.
    4   7½ in.
    5   10½ in.
    6   13½ in.
    7   18 in.

Draw lines between marks, as indicated on diagram, and cut along lines *1* and *7*. From the trimmings, cut the back piece, 8 × 4 in., neck band, and frill. The back piece and neck band need stiff interfacing.

Taking ½ in. turning, join taffeta to lining along line *1*, round off slightly at centre front. Press, turn right side out, and machine again ⅛ in. from edge. Pin or tack all round raw edges and also across centre seams, to keep both pieces absolutely true. With lining uppermost, pin or tack along marked lines *2, 3, 4, 5* and *6* (*7* is a raw edge). Machine along these lines, taking great care that the top layer does not "creep." Run a second line of stitching parallel to, and ⅜ in. from each existing line, forming casings for the boning. Machine or iron stiffening to back piece, and press all turnings inwards. Run a double gathering thread at line *7*, draw up to fit back piece, and distribute gathers evenly. Lap the back section over the gathers, pin and tack, then top-stitch on right side. Slip-stitch lining into place over raw edges.

From the left-overs, cut a 15 in. × 2 in. neckband and a lined frill 2 in. wide and up to 45 in. long. Pin a double strip of Vilene to taffeta neckband, pleat frill on to neckband, right sides together, and tack lining on top, sandwiching frill in between. Machine, and press. Tack top edge of neckband to lower edge of hood, leaving lining free. Machine along this line, but do not machine across casings—raise the presser-foot and pull the work clear, reinserting the needle on the other side of the casing. This allows the boning to be pushed down into the neckband.

Now insert boning in casings. Whalebone tends to curl, as it is stocked in a coil, and even short pieces form themselves into circles. For this reason, turn the hood inside out, and push the boning through *with* the curve. Starting at the back, insert a 27 in. length, a 29 in. length, the 31 in. length, the remaining 29 in. and finally the other 27 in. piece. Ease gathers all round, the front flange now forming a frill. Push the ends right through gaps in neckband seam and oversew the ends to the neckband turnings.

Turn hood right side out, thus reversing the thrust of the whalebone, which will now keep the calash upright, and U-shaped, instead of curling inwards. Slip-stitch lining of neck-band over raw edges and attach ribbons to neckband.

Although whalebone is more expensive than crinoline wire, it is preferable, being lighter and practically indestructible. As this is a useful stock item in the wardrobe, the extra cost is justified.

Mostly the calash was black, brown or dark green and would be worn, of course, with a cloak, which might have hand-slits, permitting a muff to be carried.

Caps also became very elaborate at this time and were frothy confections of lace and ribbon. Three or four layers of net, cut in a large circle up to 1 yard in diameter, will make an exaggera-ted mob-cap, and ribbons and lace will do the rest. Layers of net up to 12 in. wide, ruched on to ribbon and tied under the chin, also make a cap which is simple in execution and becoming in wear.

Another charming cap much affected for morning wear in the 1750's was shaped rather like a Rugby football—obviously on account of the height of coiffure over which it was worn. Choose a Terylene curtain net 36 in. wide, with a definite lateral pattern, since this provides guide lines. About 1½ yards should suffice, unless it is being worn over a monumental-sized wig.

Make a 2 in. hem on both raw edges (the short edges) and don't bother to hem the selvedges. Pin the selvedges together and, 1½ in. from the resulting centre fold, using strong, double cotton, run a single gathering thread, starting and finishing 2 in. from the hemmed edges. Leave thread-tails hanging for the time being. Repeat this operation four times, making the first two folds 12 in. from the selvedge, and the second pair 6 in. from the selvedge. This reduces the width to 20 in.; measure over wig, round the back of the head, from cheekbone to cheekbone—probably about 18 in.—and run the last two gathering threads 1 in. from selvedges. These measurements are not obligatory, and the depth of the tucks can be varied to suit individuals.

Fasten threads at one end, *firmly*, or if the gathering has been done by machine with a loose tension, tie off with a triple reef knot. Gently pull threads to gather, reducing to the required size—not including the 2 in. hem, which later forms a frilly top-knot. Secure each set of gathers with a row of machine stitching; open out the gathered strip and tweak frills into place, to stand out at right angles. (If ordinary dress net is used, cut along the folds before gathering, making a double frill.) Run a double gathering thread 2 in. from the top, by hand, on the wrong side, so that the frills are not taken in and flattened. Draw up as tightly as possible, and trim with ribbon bow. Run a ribbon through bottom hem, draw up to fit neck and tie under the chin.

The mob-cap is a circle of lawn, about 27 in. in diameter, plain for the humbler characters and edged with lace for the "ladies." Mark an inner circle 2–3 in. from the edge, and machine a bias-binding casing. Thread with elastic to fit head, and trim with contrasting ribbon and bow. These caps would sometimes also be worn under the hats, which were of felt, like the men's, or of straw. The latter can be contrived by using the wide brim of an old straw, with the crown cut down to a depth of about 2 in. trimmed with a circlet of flowers, and tied under the chin with a ribbon which comes from the edge of the brim. Towards the end of the century caps virtually disappeared, except perhaps for older characters, who might wear a lace doily with ribbons.

By 1800, hair styles had sobered down, and bonnets arrived; they stayed, in one form or another, for 100 years or so. One could fill a book on bonnets. It is only possible to suggest how to contrive a bonnet, and reference must always be made to an authoritative source for information as to size and style.

The most simple way of making a bonnet is to adapt an old straw or felt hat, or a felt hood and the cheap straw sun hats from the chain stores can be used.

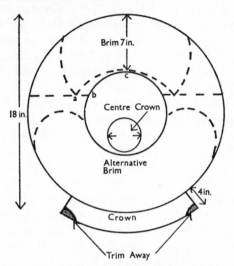

FIG. 90. POKE BONNET

Cut away the brim on a tangent across the base of the crown, hollow out slightly at the back of the neck, and round off the corners at the edge of the brim, which can then be bound and wired into the authentic poke bonnet shape, and can also be lined underneath with ruched silk or chiffon, to match the dress. Sew a straight piece of material round the outer edge and draw inwards, pleating the surplus evenly to the crown. Bind the cut edges of sun hats to prevent scratching, and add a frill at the back of the neck. Flowers, feathers, ribbons in profusion complete the creation.

Another short cut to the foundation is an esparterie "picture hat" shape which can be bought in most department stores. This can be recut, then covered in straw and the brim lined with matching silk, etc.

If a matching bonnet in fabric is required, you will need much patience, and a good supply of newspaper and Scotch tape, since cutting a pattern can be a matter of trial and error.

Two basic measurements will help; under chin to crown of head, an average of 24 in., for the brim; round nape of neck to crown of head, average 22 in., for crown of bonnet. Cut a circle of newspaper having a 9 in. radius and set aside the trimmed-off outer pieces. Fold the circle in four, and measuring from the centre point, mark a 3½ in. circle, cut away and discard. Open out the circle, and cut a 16 in. segment (measured from inner edge) as in Fig. 90, to form the brim. Trim to a crescent as indicated by dotted lines. This is the point at which a certain amount of experimentation will be necessary. By trimming away only a small piece at a–b–c, a wide-open brim will result, but by increasing the length of a–b, the brim will be brought in closer to the cheek.

The crown is cut from half of the discard. Measuring from the curved edge, pencil an outer arc about 4 in. deep, and mark on this line the measurement taken round the back of the head from nape to crown. Cut away a segment at each end (see diagram) about 2 in. deep by about 3 in. This is the point where patience and the Scotch tape will be needed. Join the crown together with a couple of paper clips and try for size. Adjust as required, tape together, then fit the brim. The easiest way to do this is to fold the brim in half at centre front, and place flat on the edge of the table. Fold the crown at the same point, and bring the two points together with the crown hanging over the edge of the table at right angles. Stick with a small piece of tape. Manoeuvre the brim and crown so that they continue to match up, always at right angles, and stick each point with tape until the cusp of the crescent marries with the crown. Turn the pattern over and repeat. This is much easier than wrestling with two opposing curves which will not lie flat without creasing the brim. Now try the paper bonnet for fit and set—the brim should stand almost at right angles to the crown at centre front, and the sides frame the cheeks.

Make all the necessary modifications in paper before cutting out the actual bonnet. The depth of brim and crown may vary, but these are the two fundamental pieces on which every bonnet is based. The crown is filled in with a circle, but it is easier to cut this when the final measurements have been decided and the actual crown cut in buckram. Join this into a circle, stand it on the buckram, and draw round it.

Put the brim together in the same way as the Tudor bonnet, make up the circular top of the crown, sandwiching the buckram between the silk and the lining, and tack all round the edge of the buckram. Join crown into a circle, also lining of crown; press inwards the turning allowance round top of crown lining and fit this to the circle, covering its raw edges. Slip-stitch together, and carefully snip the raw edges of the circle so that they lie flat.

Next, press inwards the seam allowance of the silk crown, and fit this carefully in place over the buckram, anchoring on the inside turnings with dabs of Copydex. Hold the crown in your left hand and the brim in your right hand, and starting at the left side of the bonnet, fit brim to crown, pushing the snipped raw edges of the brim to the inside of the crown. Pin in place, and stitch firmly together, using strong cotton—it won't show, as the trimming will cover the stitches. Now slide the circle with the lining attached up the inside of the crown (taking care that the neck hollow coincides) and marry the top edge of the crown to the stitched edge of the circle. The snipped turnings will thus be sandwiched away out of sight. Pin in place, and neatly stitch circle to crown; no stitches should be visible if this is meticulously done.

Make a pleated frill from a strip of silk 6 in. × 12 in. Fold long sides together, and pleat to fit the back of the neck. Stitch into place and finish off by slip-stitching the lining over all the raw edges. Trim as required.

That is the bonnet in its simplest form. After that, you can adapt it as you like.

CHAPTER EIGHT

VICTORIAN

"AND SO—Victoria." Sixty glorious years or more, during which everything, including the mantelpiece, was decently shrouded and decorated with bobbles and braid, flounces and feathers—to see Victoriana gone mad, visit Osborne House in the Isle of Wight.

From now on the wardrobe-mistress can only provide costumes for the ladies, and the men must fend for themselves; improvising and adapting, ferreting in the attic or rummaging in the second-hand shops for top hats, frock-coats, spats, malacca canes, etc. For the rest, fancy waistcoats, frilled shirts, stocks, cravats and wing collars will create an illusion which can be fostered by careful make-up in the way of beards, Dundrearys and so on, and elaborate hair styles which are almost contemporary—so does the wheel come full circle.

THE CRINOLINE

The predominant feminine outlines were governed by the crinoline, and later by the bustle; the former, though by now almost synonymous with the Victorian age, did not actually arrive until Victoria had reigned for nearly twenty years, and before that time the very voluminous skirts had been held out by numerous petticoats—six or seven of them, one of which was made of "crinoline," or horse-hair fabric, kept in shape by whalebone hoops. The metal cage-crinoline arrived about 1857, and reached its most fantastic proportions in the 1860's. Methods of making cage-crinolines are contained in a separate chapter, and provided exaggeration is avoided, there is no reason why these should not be used for costumes in the earlier years of the reign.

Dissected, the fashions turn out to be a hotch-potch of styles which not only borrow from the past, but seem to anticipate the future. Day dresses show the plain, close-fitting bodice, high neck and plain sleeves which can be adapted from any modern pattern; bodices hark back to the Normans for a loose over-sleeve, and to the Tudors for an inner sleeve of puffed, lace-trimmed lawn; for outdoor wear, the "New Look" of 1946 would have been quite the thing in 1863. Evening wear was surprisingly décolleté, with a wide neckline, completely off the shoulders.

Throughout the whole period the bodice was tight-fitting, and mostly tapering to a sharp point in the front. The Victorians went in for "separates" long before the current vogue. If this method is adopted, the separate bodice must fit very tightly, and the line be continued two inches below the waist. Otherwise, cut the bodice from the basic pattern. Use the plain sleeve pattern cut full length for a day dress, elbow length with a frill for evening wear, or the puffed sleeve mounted on a lining, as described in the Tudor chapter. The extremely wide neckline worn in the 1860's will lie better if it has an elastic slotted through it. Also, the bodice must be lined and boned. Use either whalebone strips, or old corset bones. Machine a casing of Paris binding (straight, not bias) to the bodice-lining at centre front, at bodice darts back and front, at centre back, and on side seams. Corset bones mostly have rounded ends, but if these are cut, or if whalebone is used, cover the ends with a pad of lint and sticking plaster.

Skirts can hardly be too voluminous, and six to eight yards of material is not too much, particularly with the crinoline at its full circumference. To obtain extra fullness necessary for a 3-yard crinoline, use the "standard" pattern in Fig. 29, shortening it at the back to eliminate the train. Still more fullness is gained by using the basic skirt piece (E), adapted as in Fig. 92, cutting three or even four pieces. Gather as tightly as possible (always using a double row of stitches) on to a 2 in. petersham ribbon. Cover raw edges with Paris binding.

The most effective material for evening dresses is curtain net, and it is the simplest to use; it needs no hemming and by choosing the same pattern in varying widths, the most attractive ball gowns can be made, using, for instance, three flounces of 18 in. net gathered on to a taffeta foundation. Make this of three yards of 45 in. taffeta, or three 1¼ yard lengths of 36 in. Put on the flounces before joining the side seam, as it is always easier to work flat. The lowest flounce can be about 6 yards, the next one 4 yards and the top one 3 yards. As a variation,

FIG. 91. EVENING DRESS WITH FLOUNCE SKIRT

loop up the flounces into festoons with bows. Make the bodice of satin, with tiny puffed sleeves of the net, and finish with a 6 in. deep frill round the neckline—about 1½ yards is sufficient, and the puffed sleeves can be cut from the top. If net with a finished heading is used, simply thread with ribbon and draw up to fit upper arm.

The most fashionable colour, particularly for the younger characters, was white, but this is monotonous on stage, so pastel shades can be used for the foundation and bodice, as well as for the trimmings, which can run riot—I doubt if one could think of anything which the Victorians did not think of first.

The more mature characters may be suitably upholstered in silks, satins, brocades or velvets, in strong colours, and with as much embellishment as you can pile on.

For outdoor wear, there is an endless variety of shawls,

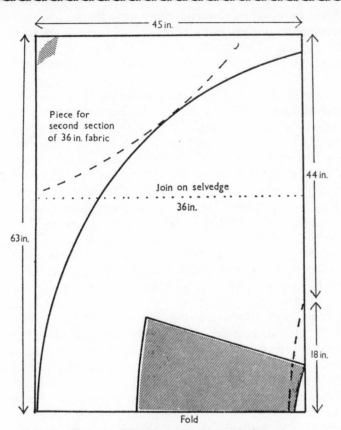

Piece for
second section
of 36 in. fabric

Join on selvedge

36 in.

45 in.

44 in.

63 in.

18 in.

Fold

FIG. 92. SECTION OF CRINOLINE SKIRT

Use two sections for medium fullness, three or four for a very full skirt.
Fabric required per section is 3½ yards of 45 in., or 3¼ yards of 36 in.

cloaks, pelerines, capes, tippets, jackets with pagoda sleeves and
so on. Capes can be of any length, and the cut and method has
already been described. From the wardrobe angle, these are
the most practical, lending themselves to a wide variety of
trimming—fur, braid, beading, what you will. The "arum
lily" collar at Fig. 23 and the flared cloak at Fig. 62 were both
copied from a Victorian cloak still in my possession—heavy
black silk plush, lined with black surah silk. This type of cloak
demonstrates the method of cutting the back seam on the cross
of the material, because it hangs so much more gracefully.

6

A variation of the cloak had very wide sleeves inset, and can be evolved from the Tudor jerkin at Fig. 41, with the bag sleeve as at Fig. 22. This cloak, as sketched, appears in the *Ladies' Treasury* of 1860 and is named "Cloak à l'Impératrice" (Fig. 93).

A hybrid of this style was the dolman mantle, which has had a revival, in a modified form, within the last decade. The cut is extremely·simple (Fig. 94), and, with suitable trimming, this is another permanent asset to the wardrobe, since the same basic pattern is also found in Edwardian fashions.

Another jacket style of the 1860's had a sudden revival, nearly 90 years later, when Dior's "New Look" came as a welcome change after the austere uniformed war years. This jacket can be cut from the basic pattern, nipped in sharply at the waist, and continued in a flare 6–8 in. deep.

By 1870 or so the crinoline made way for the bustle, which stayed in one form or another for the rest of the century. This resulted in a straight frontage from the waist downwards, with all the fullness scooped up to cascade at the back. Again, the trimmings were elaborate, but for the wardrobe mistress two simple methods emerge. The first one retains the tight-fitting bodice tapering to a point centre front (the skirt for this is based on the "standard" skirt at Fig. 29), caught up in folds a little to the rear of the side seams and attached at hip level to a less voluminous underskirt of the same, or contrasting material. There are infinite permutations—sometimes the bottom of the overskirt was turned back to reveal brocade lining which followed the fall at the back, the whole extended into a train. The main skirt will take approximately 6 yards of 45 in. material, with 3 yards cut in half lengthways to face the turn-up, to a depth of 18 inches.

The second style, which came a little later, was the elegant "princess" line. This is a little more ambitious in cut, and needs careful fitting, but in essence, it reverts to the close-fitting Plantagenet line, with seams centre back and front, and the darts extended to form seams. It is still possible to find this line in the current pattern books, since it is a classic line. If you cannot find a suitable pattern, adapt the basic pattern as at Fig. 97. This gown must fit closely on the hips, and a less exuberant bustle must be worn. The skirt flares out from knee

FIG. 93. CLOAK À L'IMPÉRATRICE

to hem, and the drapery is a separate piece, draped across the front in horizontal folds, and bunched up at the back with the ends cascading to the ground. Given the right fabric and colour, it is possible to span the centuries and use a Plantagenet gown with added draping and bodice trimming.

The fashion for the bustle held on tenaciously, until it became eventually no more than a miniature bird-cage, or half of a padded farthingale tied round the waist. Even when the bustle was discarded, the hour-glass line persisted, being achieved by an adamant corset which compelled a change of stance—pouter-pigeon bust well thrust forward, abdomen under control, and derrière well in evidence.

Once again there was a time-slip; this time sleeves reverted, and in the 1890's the leg-of-mutton or the puffed sleeve of Fig. 34, with a contrasting slash, both returned for at least a decade.

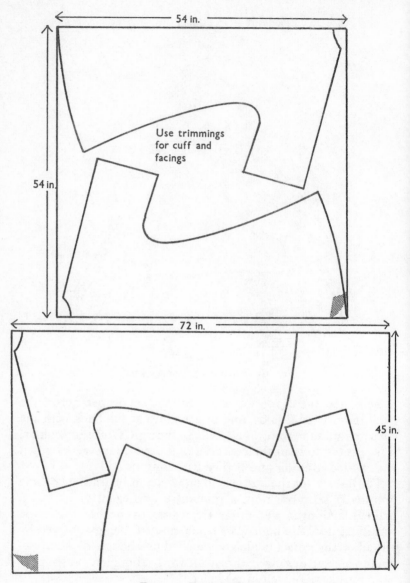

FIG. 94. DOLMAN JACKET
Above: using 3 yards of 54 in. fabric; *Below:* using 4 yards of 45 in. fabric

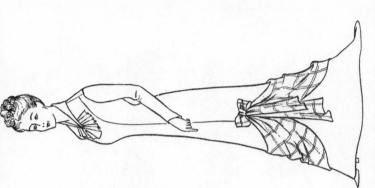

Fig. 96. Bustle Gown—Princess Line

Fig. 95. Bustle Gown with Draped Skirt

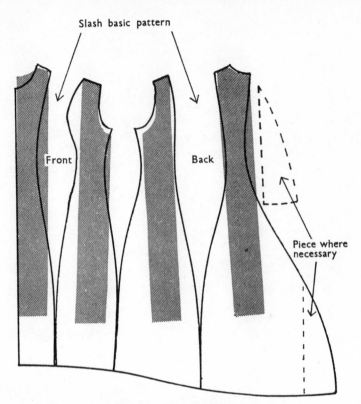

FIG. 97. PRINCESS GOWN

4½ yards of 54 in. fabric (without pile); 4½ yards of 54 in. fabric (with pile) but piece train as indicated; 5½ yards of 36 in. fabric; 6½ yards of 36 in. fabric. Use plain, close-fitting sleeve.

The 1940's "New Look" jacket was still the vogue, but skirts had changed. They were still voluminous, and ground length or even trailing, but the clumsy gathers at the waist had disappeared, and fullness was achieved by gores, which make for more economical cutting, as shown in Fig. 98.

Four dramatists frequently performed come into this fin-de-siècle period: Pinero, Wilde, Chekhov and Shaw. The dressing of this era is quite fascinating and need not be too extravagant. For day wear a basic suit can be teamed up with different blouses and hats. The blouses provide interesting variety: the plainest was the classic "shirt" blouse, with a modest puff to

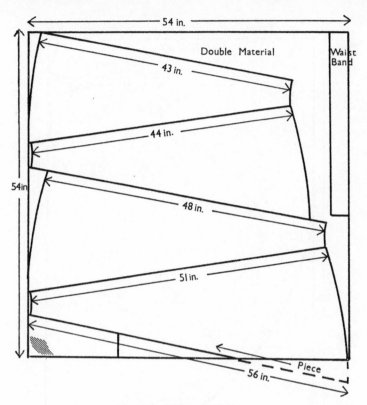

FIG. 98. 8-GORED SKIRT
Using 3 yards of 54 in. fabric

the sleeve; the more elaborate were tucked and frilled, lace-trimmed, and beribboned.

Evening dress offers enormous scope. Trains may be as long as the player can manage, and the "standard" skirt of Fig. 29 can be adapted. Since the skirt must fit smoothly over the hips, the fullness at the waist must be eliminated. This can be done by cutting as in Fig. 99.

Bodices were tight fitting, with a normal waist-line, and can be cut on the same lines as before; the pointed front, perhaps the most persistent line in the history of dress, remained in vogue. Sleeves were either puffed, or just a fall of lace, accordion-pleated silk, or a fringe. A half-circle of material having a

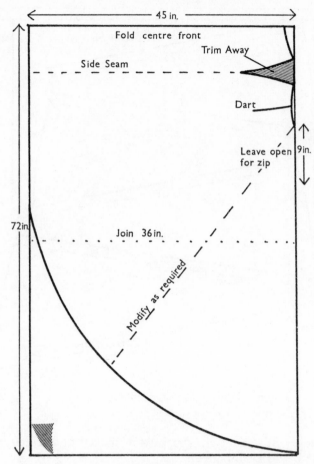

FIG. 99. STANDARD SKIRT ADAPTED FOR 1890's
Using 4 yards of 45 in. fabric or 5 yards of 36 in. For the modified skirt
use 3 yards of 36 in. fabric

diameter equal to the arm-hole measurement, makes a simple and graceful finish.

Perhaps the most typical accessory, however, which will pinpoint this era, is the boned lace collar (see Fig. 100). It fitted closely to the throat, under the chin, up to the ears, fastening at the back with minute hooks and loops or tiny press-studs. At the base of the neck it was joined to a matching lace gilet which

FIG. 100. LADIES' SUIT WITH LONG JACKET AND, INSET, HIGH-
BONED LACE COLLAR AND JABOT

fastened under the bodice. This was another fashion which had
a very long run, and I can even recall its being worn in the
1920's by the more conservative. Like the wimple, it is very
becoming, and is easy to make, being a straight piece of lace,
folded double or backed with fine net. Take the measurement
from the base of the neck to the hollow behind the ear lobe,
and mark this point for insertion of the bones, which can be of
ribbon wire or feather-boning (it is unlikely that even the most
old-fashioned shop will still have the proper little wires). Curve

the top slightly to fit down under the chin, and make to fit without wrinkles. Instead of the "gilet," a jabot can be attached, of either pleated lawn or net—the one in the illustration (Fig. 100) was a straight piece of frilling, doubled in half and drawn up tightly with a gathering thread, then pulled apart to form a fan.

HATS AND BONNETS

The bonnets and hats which featured in the pages of the ladies' journals of the time ranged from miniature to monster,

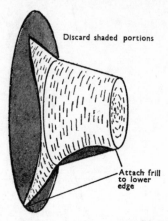

Discard shaded portions

Attach frill
to lower
edge

FIG. 101. BONNET ADAPTED FROM STRAW HAT

and feathers, flowers, fruit, lace and ribbons were all used to decorate them.

The method described in Chapter Seven can still be followed, the size being dictated by a careful reference to the authorities.

By following the instructions for making the calash, with a modification in the boning, a delightful early Victorian bonnet can be evolved. The back piece is a complete circle, and main piece is reduced to about 13 inches at its widest (plus, of course, turnings' allowances). Mark out the lining in the same way, but omit the frill by bringing the row of machining for the casing $\frac{3}{8}$ in. from the edge. The deep bottom frill goes across the back only. Use shorter lengths of whalebone, drawing in the fullness to frame the face, and this time insert it so that it curves inwards.

Using the same method, cut three 16-inch (approximate)

strips to fit closely to the head, for the crown, but push out the
edge into a brim, with a strip approximately 27 in. or more,
according to the width of brim required, adjusting the interval
between casings accordingly.

Bonnets were at their smallest when crinolines were at their
widest, giving a pyramid silhouette, and contemporary with
the Cloak à l'Impératrice, the *Ladies' Treasury* shows the bonnet
in Fig. 93. This is the bonnet at its simplest in actual form, and
seems to have been chiefly of straw, with a frill at the neck, and
the usual multifarious trimmings. The easiest way to make
this is to cut down an old straw hat, using one with a fairly deep
crown. Trim away as indicated at Fig. 101, wire the front edge,
and bend the points of the crescent forward. Attach the frill
to the lower edge, tapering it to nothing at the points; insert a
ruche of net or lace under the brim, and complete with trimmings as desired.

With the advent of the bustle and consequent change of
silhouette, the bonnet found a rival in the hat, at first of the
"carnival novelty" size, worn tilted over the forehead. This
can be contrived in a number of ways, using a child's shallow-
crowned hat as a foundation. By the 1890's hats were larger,
perched on top of high, upswept coiffures, and veiling was very
fashionable, remaining so right up till the outbreak of war in
1914. The hat was secured to the top-knot with a 12-inch hat-
pin; the veil was then arranged round the brim, over the face,
pulled taut under the chin and taken up to tie at the back of
the crown.

All the costumes of the Victorian as well as the Edwardian
eras, depend for their effectiveness on profuse ornamentation,
and the wardrobe mistress often does very well by asking some
of the older members of the company for whatever they may
have hidden away in drawer or attic.

This may seem a surprisingly brief and sketchy review of such
a long and varied array of fashion; but apart from the crinoline
and bustle, dealt with in a separate chapter, what remains is
really covered in previous chapters, and repetition is pointless.

One major difference must be noted, however. Until
Victorian times, children were more or less miniature replicas
of their elders. It is beyond the scope of this book to go into the

changes which then emerge, and reference must be made to the appropriate books. The girls present less of a problem, however. They simply wore a small hoop, under a skirt slightly above ankle length, and long white drawers trimmed with *broderie anglaise* or lace.

CHAPTER NINE

THE EDWARDIAN ERA
THE GREAT WAR
THE TWENTIES AND THIRTIES

"THE Edwardians"—gay and graceful, theirs was an almost legendary world so near in time yet so remote in dress and manners. Dresses still swept the ground, but for the last time, except for formal evening wear.

As with the turn-of-the-century costume, the coat-and-skirt with blouses is the most practical way of dealing with most productions, and hats offer great scope for imagination. They were wide enough to make the prevailing silhouette almost T-shaped, and sat fairly and squarely on the top of the head. One might wonder, seeing the carefully preserved examples in the dress museums, why the very large crowns did not extinguish the wearer. The secret was in the "bandeau," a wired circle of velvet rather like a tea plate minus its middle. This was stitched inside the hat at the junction of brim and crown, and provided a "plateau" which rested on the crown of the head. The balance of these elaborate affairs is hazardous, and once again the Alice-band comes into service; this, with a firmly tied veil, gives a degree of confidence—for the rest, keep your head up and remember you are a lady.

Evening dress was elaborate, sometimes making use of yards and yards of accordion-pleated chiffon. Basically, the cutting is simplified to a plain fitted bodice with the "standard skirt" falling into a train. An elegant trimming can be made using a triangular insert at the hem or a pleated contrast, which can be repeated as a short cap sleeve.

Most of these dresses look more effective with a little discreet padding at the hips to accentuate the smallness of the waist. Bosoms were ample and well upholstered—none of the perky post-war little "falsies" but good solid padding, with a triangular piece to bridge the gap and present an unbroken facade.

Gradually hips became more slender, and a typical "gimmick" of the day was the "hobble" skirt. This is a style to

FIG. 102. DRESS WITH "PEG-TOP" SKIRT

which it is not practical to adhere too closely, but the effect can be achieved by careful drapery as in Fig. 102, using about 3 yards of 45 in. material. Very little cutting is necessary, and a useful length will remain for future use.

Make a 2 in. petersham waistband, and work "on the model" with the fastening to the left. Pin the halfway mark of the material to the centre back, then continue each way to the side seam. Now measure about 25 in. along the selvedge, and bring this point back in a loop to the side seam—this will make a downward fold to give the peg-top effect; there is no need to join up as the drape will conceal the edge. Repeat at the left side, and this will allow the skirt to be unfastened, leaving enough room to get out of it. With the model facing you, take

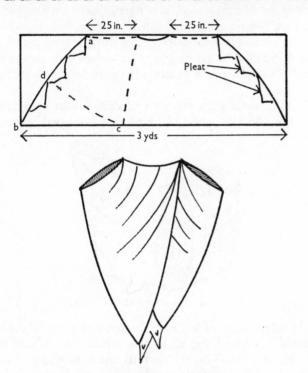

FIG. 103. "PEG-TOP" SKIRT

your right-hand lower corner and pin to the model's right seam-point. Tuck in the top point (from side seam to lower edge) and arrange the surplus fullness to fall in deep folds from waist to hem. This is a matter of careful adjustment, and it is worth taking time to achieve the right effect. Then take the opposite corner (your left-hand side), pin to model's left, and again arrange surplus. The swathe will then be quite close-fitting at the ankles.

Remove skirt and sew firmly to waist-band.

The wearer will need to move and sit carefully in this skirt, and concealed tacks are necessary, to prevent the front falling open. Wear a straight waist slip about 4 in. shorter than the skirt, and take small steps. *The Wearing of Costume** gives useful guidance.

* See list of useful books, p. 162.

If made in thin material, it is hardly necessary to cut away the surplus, *a–b* on diagram; if thicker material is used—dress woollen, for a suit, for instance, make the side loop smaller, and trim on line *c–d*, *after* arranging pleats to see how much surplus there is. Point *d* is taken to the side seam, and *a–d* arranged in folds.

The hat to wear with this style of skirt would be a "toque," so that the silhouette would be diamond-shaped. Fig. 104 is

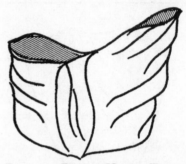

FIG. 104. DRAPED VELVET TOQUE

a simple adaptation of a toque featured in a 1912 magazine. Use an old hat or a "shape" having a rolled brim, and swathe this in velvet, pulling up the surplus either side into "ears."

The 1914–1918 war chopped inches off hems, and skirts became much fuller. Waist-lines were normal, and there is nothing which requires intricate cutting. Present day patterns can be adapted.

The early Twenties were sloppy and shapeless, and gradually "The Girl Friend" emerged—skinny as a bean pole, minus bust and bottom, and skirts at their shortest ever—until the time of writing this book, when mini-skirts and micro-mini's are the rage.

Waistlines suddenly slid down round the hips, so that in 1927/28, the skirt was shorter than the bodice. A very slight extra fullness was either pleated or gauged to the bodice, and later embellishments were trailing sashes, and "handkerchief" over-skirts, giving an uneven hem-line to break the monotony. The basic sheath pattern can be used—slash 8–9 in. below the waist and cut skirt very slightly fuller, adding no more than half to the original width.

By cutting the bodice slightly longer, and mounting it on a lining, a slightly bloused effect is achieved—fashionable round about 1929. Fringed overskirts were also worn especially in the "Charleston" era.

Necklines were very plain, slightly boat-shaped; summer and evening dresses were sleeveless, and both day and evening dresses were short.

Coats were tubular wrap-overs, with large fur collars, and sometimes fur cuffs and hemlines. The only hat shape possible with such a collar was the "cloche," which was worn jammed down to the eyebrows, with a small turned-up brim in front and none at all at the back.

About 1931, we found our skirts round our ankles—almost overnight, it seemed. The waist line was back to normal, the "cloche" was out, and hats were very shallow, tilted over the one eye. In the mid-thirties the leg-of-mutton sleeve had a sudden revival, and another very fashionable line was the sharp *upward* point of the skirt front. Skirts gradually went up to mid-calf for day wear, but evening dress remained floor length, even for informal dances.

The war brought a degree of austerity never before known, and the "sumptuary laws" came back in a different form. Controls, extending even to "the little woman round the corner" were strict, and clothes rationing put a brake on fashion changes. The "line" was practically square, in imitation of the Service uniforms, though tailored suits were very definitely waisted.

No book on costume can ever be completely up to date; ever Dior's "New Look" is now a museum piece. There are rustlings of skirts, but only one thing is certain—fashion, like the weather, is changeable, capricious, intriguing—a perennial talking-point.

CHAPTER TEN

FARTHINGALES HOOPS CRINOLINES BUSTLES

THE farthingale arrived with Katharine of Aragon, and in one form or another stayed until about the middle of the nineteenth century. Its silhouette changed, of course, but all the variations can be modified, and a basic all-purpose petticoat can be evolved, merely by adding or removing hoops, and bending as required.

Three yards is a practical circumference. Anything larger can prove an embarrassment on a small stage, particularly when making entrances and exits—even this modest hoop will have a diameter of 35 in., which is wider than the average door, so it is always wise to check these points before deciding on the actual size. Another point which must be considered is length. The lowest hoop must always clear the instep, and in fact, barely ankle length is safer. (The skirt, of course, may reach the ground and even trail at the back.) For this reason, 36 in. fabric is quite adequate, and can be shortened as required. The basic method is the same.

Take three yards of strong, close-weave material—calico, glazed cotton, gingham (the latter, with a check or line to follow, provides useful "guide lines"). Cut from the long side a strip 9 in. wide, and shorten this to $1\frac{3}{4}$ yards (63 in.). Seam together the short edges to form circles. Along the raw edge of the lower section (larger piece) form 16 flat pleats $1\frac{1}{4}$ in. deep (that is, insert two upright pins $2\frac{1}{2}$ in. apart, and bring them together to make pleat). Space these pleats about $3\frac{1}{2}$ in. apart, thus reducing the lower skirt to the same size (more or less) as the upper section. Tack this raw edge $\frac{1}{4}$ in. below the selvedge of the upper section and machine $\frac{5}{8}$ in. from the edge. (Make sure that all the pleats lie in the same direction, otherwise you will have difficulty in inserting the wire.) Press both edges downwards, and machine along the selvedge to form the casing for the first hoop, leaving free about 2 in. through which to push the wire. Finish with a $\frac{1}{2}$ in. hem at the waist and thread with wide *tape* (not elastic, since the gathers have to be variously spaced, and this is not easy with elastic). Make the bottom hem ⅝ in. deep and leave a similar opening for the wire.

This is the basic petticoat.

The early Tudor silhouette was cone-shaped, and only the bottom hoop is required. Later, in Elizabethan costume, the hips were rounded by the addition of padding. Make a pair of crescent-shaped pads, the distance between the points being half the waist measurement, and the depth up to about 7 in. (Fig. 105). Cut four sections from strong cotton material, and join to form two bags, leaving open a short section on upper edge through which to insert the padding. Stuff firmly with foam rubber crumbs or kapok, sew up slit, and attach tapes to each point, so that a single pad can, when necessary, be used as a bustle.

Next, the farthingale resembled a cartwheel, from about 1588 until about 1620. To modify the basic petticoat, remove the bottom hoop; shorten the centre front of top section to about 3 in. by a single deep pleat or by a very strong double gathering thread. Insert a hoop of 66 in. in the top casing (see later note about wire); after tying tape firmly at waist, shift all the gathers to the back. This has the effect of flattening the front skirt to take the stomacher, and pushes the hoop backwards to give the cartwheel line, with the "hub" slightly off-centre.

This type of farthingale went out of fashion after the death of Anne of Denmark, but hip pads or rolls were still worn; these can be used, in a suitably modified form, for any costume up to about the reign of Queen Anne, and reference to the costume books gives guidance as to size.

The new hoop (which was worn from the early 1700's until about 1780, when the bustle came into vogue) was elliptical, with the width at the sides. To achieve this, push the gathers equally to the sides; shorten top section centre front and centre back, as described above (Fig. 106). Use only the top hoop, and refer to the costume books for guidance on the degree of flattening necessary—the hoop became progressively wider from side to side and narrower from back to front. (See later note regarding the uses of different kinds of wire.)

Next comes the crinoline, for which three hoops are used, one at the top, one threaded through the bottom hem, and one

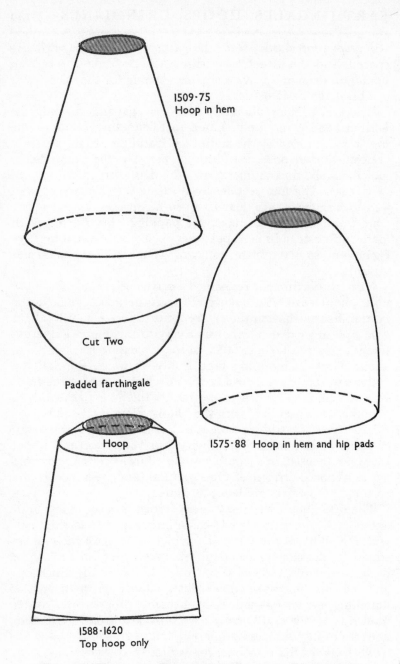

1509·75
Hoop in hem

Cut Two

Padded farthingale

1575·88 Hoop in hem and hip pads

Hoop

1588·1620
Top hoop only

FIG. 105. TUDOR AND ELIZABETHAN HOOPS AND FARTHINGALES

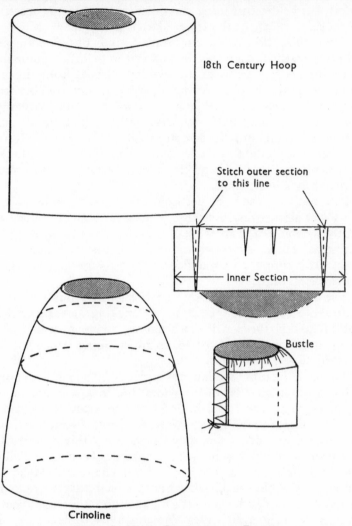

18th Century Hoop

Stitch outer section
to this line

←————— Inner Section —————→

Bustle

Crinoline

FIG. 106. HOOP, CRINOLINE AND BUSTLE

in between. The exact placing of this centre hoop depends
upon the wearer—it should be 1 in. above fingertip level, so
that if the wearer has to sit down, she can unobtrusively slide
both hands behind her back and lift both hoops as she sits
(Fig. 106).

Make this centre hoop about 2¼ yards in circumference, and

insert this before threading the other two. It is not necessary
to make a casing, as the lower skirt is not shaped. Mark the
position all round with tacking thread, chalk or ball-point pen,
fold the top inwards to this line, and press to form a guide line.
Slide the hoop in between the two layers, hold firmly in position, and stitch in place by hand, using strong double cotton
and taking fairly small stitches, not more than ¼ in. When you
have stitched about half way, ease some of the fullness round
the wire, but do not pull the cotton tight, otherwise it will snap
in wear. Continue full circle, and the surplus will work itself
into small gathers all round the hoop. Insert top and bottom
hoops in existing casings.

Alternatively, the basic petticoat can be modified by halving
the lower skirt, using the same method as above; reduce the
centre section to 2¼ yards, pleat bottom section to fit, and form
casing as before. Although the real crinoline had many more
hoops, this simplified three-decker serves very well and gives
the authentic line.

The hoop's final form was the bustle, and this requires a
little more contriving. It is no use making a petticoat with
half-hoops, as these will immediately swing forward. The
hoops must be firmly fixed to an inner lining which in turn
must fit closely from waist to hips.

To make the inner section, cut a piece of strong cotton fabric
equal to three-quarters of the widest hip measurement (about
30 in. average) and equal in depth to the wearer's suspender-
belt or roll-on (about 13 in. average). Mark 6½ in. from each
short edge, and draw a perpendicular line—this is where the
side seam would be. Mark ¾ in. either side of each line, fold on
line, and make dart 7 in. deep, to form side seam. Make two
more darts at the back, where normal skirt darts would be.
Hollow out to a depth of about 1 in. back and front, as indicated
on diagram (Fig. 106). Press front turnings to *right* side, and
machine Rufflette tape down each front edge (remove gathering
strings).

Cut outer section 13½ in. × 31 in., having, if possible, a
selvedge on the long edge. Turn up a ⅝ in. hem, and leave the
middle 4 in. open. Machine a casing 4½ in. from top, and
again, leave open 4 in. at centre back.

Trim away as indicated on diagram, 1½ in. at waist edge,

FIG. 107. BASIC SHAPES: *Left*, TUDOR; *Right*, CARTWHEEL
FARTHINGALE

tapering to nothing at bottom edge. Press $\frac{1}{2}$ in. seam allowance inwards, and top-stitch to inner section along side-seam line. Pleat in the fullness at the waist edge and machine to waist edge of inner section; turn in $\frac{1}{2}$ in. and machine Paris Binding over raw edges.

Cut two pieces of wire, 30 in. for the lower edge and 27 in. for the upper casing. Bend carefully and insert through open slits; finish off slits by hand. This is easier than inserting wires before machining inner and outer sections, as the wires will fight the machine needle.

Lace across the front with a 2-yard stay lace, otherwise a pair of wide bootlaces tied together. This is better than tape, which will go stringy, and cut.

Here again, the real bustle was a far more elaborate affair, but this makes a very firm and effective bustle, and if tightly laced, it will not shift in wear. The lacing provides for variations in measurements, but if a bustle is to remain one person's property, the inner section can be omitted, and the outer section machined firmly to her roll-on, suspender belt or other foundation garment. Alternative fastenings can be made from

FIG. 108. BASIC SHAPES: EIGHTEENTH CENTURY HOOP

FIG. 109. BASIC SHAPES: *Left*, CRINOLINE; *Right*, BUSTLE

wide elastic and hooked tape which can be bought by the yard or taken off old belts or bras. The important point is to achieve a tight fit.

For a smaller bustle, use half the Elizabethan hip pad.

Proper crinoline wire is not expensive, and is preferable if any extensive use is contemplated. It is obtainable in widths of $\frac{3}{16}$ in., $\frac{3}{8}$ in. and $\frac{5}{8}$ in., according to the weight of skirt it has to carry. The middle size, $\frac{3}{8}$ in., will generally be found suitable, but if either of the other sizes is used, the width of the casing must be varied accordingly. The wire is flexible, and its own thrust will keep it in place once it has been inserted in the casing; a 3 in. overlap must always be allowed, and this should be pushed some distance beyond the opening, to prevent the ends from sticking out. The wire is cased in cotton, and the ends need to be covered by plaster, to prevent fraying, and possible cutting of the petticoat. If this kind of wire is used for the crinoline, it is essential either to bind the ends together into a circle for the middle hoop, before sewing into the skirt, or to make the middle casing of the correct size, as described above, otherwise the spring will push the ends apart and spoil the line.

As a very much cheaper alternative, 12-gauge galvanized wire can be used. This can be bought in coils of 1 pound, giving about 11 yards, for about 2s. a coil at the time of writing (compared with 1s. 6d. per yard for crinoline wire), so that even allowing for future inevitable price increases, this will always be cheaper. Its disadvantages are that it has no "spring," and having achieved a perfect circle, care must be taken not to knock it out of true. Double wire is preferable, particularly for the bottom hoop of the Tudor or crinoline petticoat, and for the cartwheel farthingale and Hanoverian hoop. (For the latter, it is preferable to real crinoline wire, as it will hold its elliptical shape without cross ties.)

Hammer flat 2 in. of the cut ends, overlap, and bind firmly with sticking plaster, insulation tape, or Sellotape X, not ordinary Scotch tape. When making the Hanoverian hoop, thread wire in the round, and bind both hoops together at the opening—a bit awkward, but not impossible. The hoop can then be pulled into shape.

Another method is to make a separate casing of tape, wide enough to carry two strands of wire. Thread the wire, push clear of ends, bind together as above, then draw the casing over the join and sew together. The hoops can then be sewn inside the petticoat as required, and as galvanized wire will stand a considerable amount of bending, the same hoop will do for either cartwheel or Hanoverian styles, provided sharp kinks are avoided.

Real crinoline wire is better for the bustle. Galvanized wire can be used, but if it is inserted from the middle, it will have to be bent carefully into shape afterwards, and the raw ends must be well bound to prevent them from pushing through the casing.

NOTE. The easiest way to cope with any hoop or farthingale is to put on the *dress* first and then step into the petticoat, rather than put on the petticoat first and struggle with a voluminous gown. This avoids disturbing make-up.

It is also essential to get used to wearing a hoop, and at as many rehearsals as possible, wear a hoop with a full length petticoat. Even if no hoop is being worn, it is better to become accustomed to moving in a trailing skirt.

CHAPTER ELEVEN

DYEING AND STRIPPING

THE distinction between dyeing and dipping is that the former entails boiling, and results in a faster, stronger colour which, however, does not strip so easily. Dipping is satisfactory with quite a number of fabrics, and will strip very easily and quickly, for re-dyeing. Use more dye and less water, as dipping will not give such a strong colour.

The initial steps are the same. Follow the maker's instructions as to preparing dye, allowing a sufficient amount for the weight of material. Dissolve the dye thoroughly in boiling water—an old enamel saucepan is the best thing for this. If the material has to be simmered, do this in a large enamel pan or a galvanized bath, large enough to allow the material to be stirred and kept moving. For dipping, the water should be nearly boiling, but the simmering is omitted, and there is no need to rinse, as this washes out some of the colour and makes the colour paler.

Notes on various fabrics:

WOOL—not easy to dye; will not "take" unless simmered.

HESSIAN—takes colour well, without streaking. It is not necessary to boil it. It is easier to cut out the garment first, and dip the pieces in a receptacle large enough to obviate too much folding. Wet the hessian thoroughly, prepare a strong solution, and make sure the pieces are thoroughly saturated. Agitate as little as possible, as hessian frays. Drip dry, without creasing.

VELVET—the easiest of any material to dye. Furnishing velour or cotton velveteen takes more evenly, quickly and with completely true colour than any other material. Always dip, never wring, hang straight and drip dry. Will also strip and re-dye well.

TAFFETA—not worth trying, in view of cheapness and wide colour range. Creases very easily when wet and retains creases even after careful ironing. Difficult to dye without streaking; if attempted, must be drip dried, completely stretched.

RAYON SATIN—as taffeta.

RAYON CREPE-DE-CHINE—very amenable. No need to simmer, takes colour without streaking, will strip and re-dye. I used one length for four different costumes; the original one, which had been shaded with dye, was stripped and dyed red. This was later stripped and dyed lavender, stripped again and dyed pink.

SPUN RAYON ("Moygashel" type weave)—needs soaking, as it is slow to take colour, but need not be simmered unless deep colour is required. Frays and needs careful handling.

BOLTON TWILL SHEETING—this is a very useful material as to width, hang and body, suitable for cloaks and tunics. Takes dye well, and will dip, provided extra dye is used. Strips completely, if only dipped. Frays quickly so needs careful handling.

WINCEYETTE—not very satisfactory, but if necessary, can be tinted by adding dye to flame-proofing solution.

The most unsatisfactory material I ever tried to dye was a very fine, closely woven cotton. After boiling, it eventually took the colour, but did not look good, and acquired permanent creases and streaks.

These notes are based on the use of ordinary household dyes such as Drummer, which I always found very satisfactory, or Dylon, which is a little more expensive. Aniline dye, though good for large quantities of material for use as drapes, must not be used for costumes, as it rubs off on the skin even when fixed with Glauber Salts.

As regards colour changes, unless you are starting with white, take into account the resultant blend. Even the palest shade will have an effect, and it is better to dip a small piece of the material first. The instruction leaflets in the dye packets give clear instructions on this point.

It is almost impossible to achieve a deep, pure black, and brown is also difficult, except with velveteen.

Stripping is much less drastic than it sounds. The fabric will not disintegrate before your eyes—I only once succeeded in bleaching a piece of material to rotting point, and that was a sun-fast casement cotton steeped in undiluted bleach.

For the more delicate materials, use Dygon or Drummer Colour Remover, in the proportions and according to makers' instructions. It is, however, rather expensive to use these on a large scale, and ordinary household bleach is safe enough, *provided always* that the material is very thoroughly rinsed until there is no trace of bleach smell. The bleach must be used in a fairly strong concentration, and one bottle to a (bathroom) bath of hot water, about 6 in. deep, will do a very efficient job. Obstinate colour may be left to soak, stirring from time to time to prevent streaking. If material has only been dipped, the colour comes out almost in minutes.

Bleaching will not always give a pure white, but will remove enough colour to make it possible to re-dye to almost any reasonably strong shade. The cardinal point to remember is the rinsing, since any residue of bleach will counteract re-dyeing.

I used this system consistently for tights, since it is not practicable to buy new ones for each production. Starting with white cotton tights, which are not expensive, it is possible to use them for a whole series—I cannot recollect that the holes resulted from bleaching, but only from nails in the set.

Since stretch tights have come into general wear, there is quite a wide range of colours available, but it is not advisable to try to strip and re-dye these.

INDEX

(Page numbers in Italics refer to illustrations and diagrams.)